4 WorkplacePlus

Living and Working in English

Joan Saslow

Workbook by
Barbara R. Denman

Workplace Plus: Living and Working in English 4
Workbook

Copyright © 2004 by Pearson Education, Inc.
All rights reserved.

Pearson Education, 10 Bank Street, White Plains, NY 10606

Senior acquisitions editor: Marian Wassner
Development editor: Trish Lattanzio
Senior production editor: Robert Ruvo
Marketing manager: Oliva Fernandez
Senior manufacturing buyer: Nancy Flaggman
Cover and Text design: Ann France
Text composition: Word & Image Design Studio Inc.
Text font: Palatino
Illustrations: Brian Hughes, pp. 19, 24, 31, 34, 90, 93, 95, 97;
    NSV Productions, pp. 6, 15, 30, 46, 48, 54, 70, 85-87, 91, 100;
    Dusan Petricic, pp. 3, 22, 83; Meryl Treatner, p. 71;
    Word & Image, pp. 8, 22

ISBN: 0-13-094352-5

Printed in the United States of America
    6 7 8 9 10–BAH–11 10 09 08

Contents

Unit 1 Your life and work ○○○○○○○○○○○○○○○○○○○○○○○○○○○○○○○○○○○○○ 1

Unit 2 Your environment ○○○○○○○○○○○○○○○○○○○○○○○○○○○○○○○○○○ 9

Unit 3 Your equipment and machines ○○○○○○○○○○○○○○○○○○○○○○○ 17

Unit 4 Your customers ○○○○○○○○○○○○○○○○○○○○○○○○○○○○○○○○○○○○○ 25

Unit 5 Your time ○○ 33

Unit 6 Your supplies and resources ○○○○○○○○○○○○○○○○○○○○○○○○○ 41

Unit 7 Your relationships ○○○○○○○○○○○○○○○○○○○○○○○○○○○○○○○○○○○ 49

Unit 8 Your health and safety ○○○○○○○○○○○○○○○○○○○○○○○○○○○○○ 57

Unit 9 Your money ○○ 65

Unit 10 Your career ○○○○○○○○○○○○○○○○○○○○○○○○○○○○○○○○○○○○○○○ 73

Skills for test taking ○○○○○○○○○○○○○○○○○○○○○○○○○○○○○○○○○○○○○○ 81

UNIT 1

Your life and work

➤ Practical conversations

1 **➤ VOCABULARY** Match the pictures and the sentences. Write the letter on the line.

1.  _____

2.  _____

3.  _____

4.  _____

5.  _____

a. I'd be happy to make some phone calls.

b. I offered to distribute flyers for the car wash.

c. The school is having a bake sale on Saturday

d. Alfredo volunteers at the homeless shelter.

e. Would you be willing to make a donation?

2 Have you ever been asked to do one of these volunteer activities? Check ☑ <u>yes</u> or <u>no</u>.

	yes	no
1. Donate books for a book sale.	❏	❏
2. Volunteer at an animal shelter.	❏	❏
3. Give canned food to a food pantry.	❏	❏
4. Make a money donation.	❏	❏
5. Donate clothing to a homeless shelter.	❏	❏
6. Offer to mail some letters.	❏	❏

3 Complete the conversation. Use words from the box.

calling	interested	busy	speak	time	flyers	loans	send

A: Good evening. May I please _____ to Mr. Armstrong?
1.

B: This is Mr. Armstrong.

A: Hello, sir. My name is Myra Apple and I'm _____ from First City Bank
2.

to tell you about our special offer on _____ this month.
3.

B: I'm sorry. I'm _____ right now.
4.

A: I understand. May I _____ you one of our _____ instead?
5.   6.

B: No thanks. I'm really not _____.
7.

A: OK. Thank you for your _____.
8.

4 Complete the conversations. Use your <u>own</u> words.

1. **A:** I'd like to get involved in some volunteer work. Tell me, _____, do

   you volunteer?

   B: Yes, I do. I _____.

   A: _____. Do they need any more help?

   B: Yes, they do. Would you be willing to _____?

   A: _____.

2. **A:** Good afternoon. May I speak to _____?

   B: Who's calling, please?

   A: This is _____. I'm calling from _____

   about _____.

   B: Is this a sales call?

   A: Yes, it is.

   B: I'm sorry. _____.

   A: _____.

➤ Practical grammar

5 **Complete each sentence with the simple present tense or the present continuous.**

1. I usually _____ a few hours every week at my son's school.
   <u>volunteer / am volunteering</u>

2. This week, the mail carriers _____ for the food pantry.
   <u>collect / are collecting</u>

3. When a telemarketer calls, I _____ to be polite.
   <u>try / am trying</u>

4. Sometimes good causes _____ telemarketers too.
   <u>use / are using</u>

5. The Music Club _____ a bake sale at the soccer game this Saturday.
   <u>has / is having</u>

6. We _____ donations for Alicia's family. Their apartment burned
   <u>take / are taking</u>

   down last week.

6 **Complete each sentence with the simple present tense or the present continuous. Use verbs from the box.**

wait	be	take	help
~~ask~~	come	call	

"Good evening. This is the third day of our March Pledge Drive here at XPTV,

your public television station. This week we _**are asking**_ you to pledge a donation to
                                              1.

support public TV. Your donations _____ us bring you the programs you love.
                                        2.

When you _____ a volunteer will take your name and credit card information.
              3.

It only _____ about 90 seconds. You can pledge online too. Our Web site
             4.

_____ secure and easy to use. We only _____ to you twice a year, so
      5.   6.

call and pledge now! Our volunteers _____ call to hear from you!"
                                          7.

7 Complete the conversation with the simple present tense or the present continuous.

A: Hey, Maria. What's up?

B: I _____ these clothes to the homeless shelter. I _____ things
    <u>1. take / am taking</u>   <u>2. donate / am donating</u>

   to them once a month.

A: That's terrific. You know, I _____ to do more volunteer work. Do you
                                   <u>3. try / am trying</u>

   think they _____ more donations?
               <u>4. want / are wanting</u>

B: Sure. Right now they _____ clothes women can wear to a job interview.
                      <u>5. need / are needing</u>

   Things like suits, skirts, and blouses.

A: I'm sure I _____ some clothes like that at home. I'll take a look tonight.
           <u>6. have / am having</u>

B: Great! I'm sure they'll appreciate it.

8 ▶ *CHALLENGE* Look at the answers. Complete the questions. Use the simple present
tense or the present continuous

1. Why _*do you donate money to that charity*_____?

   I donate money to that charity because it's a good cause.

2. What _____?

   I'm baking cookies for the bake sale right now.

3. Where _____?

   I want to go to the benefit concert tonight.

4. Who _____?

   Hami and Penny are running the car wash on Saturday.

5. What _____?

   I tell telemarketers that I don't take sales offers over the phone.

9 Complete the sentence about <u>yourself</u>.

1. On Friday, I _____.

2. When a telemarketer calls, I _____.

3. _____ this weekend.

➤ Authentic practice

🔟 Read. Choose your response. Fill in the ovals.

1. "Would you be willing to contribute to the scholarship fund?"

   ⓐ We already have one.　　　　　ⓑ With pleasure.

2. "What time can I stop by to drop off the flyers?"

   ⓐ Is 6:00 OK?　　　　　ⓑ A million!

3. "You could help run the car wash."

   ⓐ When is it?　　　　　ⓑ Is this a sales call?

4. "I'm going to be out of town for a few days."

   ⓐ There you go!　　　　　ⓑ I understand.

5. "Who should I make the check payable to?"

   ⓐ Make it out to the Main Street　　　　　ⓑ Better come early!
   Homeless Shelter.

1️⃣1️⃣ Complete the conversation. Write the letter on the line.

1. What do you want to do tonight? ____

2. What's the Sip and Sing? ____

3. Sounds fun. How much is
   the admission? ____

4. What if I don't want dessert? ____

5. It sounds like a good cause. What time
   does it start? ____

a. It's free, but you pay for the
   desserts and coffee. It's a
   fundraiser for the youth
   center.

b. At 7:00 p.m.

c. You could make a cash
   contribution instead.

d. Let's go to the community
   center for the Sip and Sing.

e. It's a talent show they do
   every Friday night.

12 **Read the information from the Federal Trade Commission's Web site.**

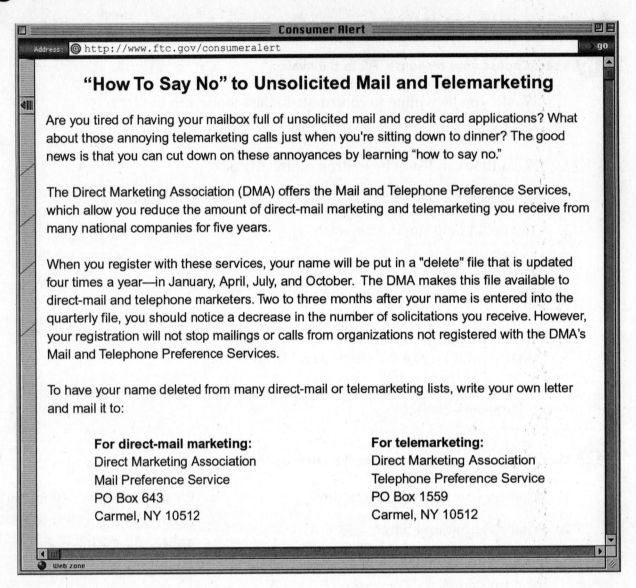

Consumer Alert

Address: @ http://www.ftc.gov/consumeralert   go

"How To Say No" to Unsolicited Mail and Telemarketing

Are you tired of having your mailbox full of unsolicited mail and credit card applications? What about those annoying telemarketing calls just when you're sitting down to dinner? The good news is that you can cut down on these annoyances by learning "how to say no."

The Direct Marketing Association (DMA) offers the Mail and Telephone Preference Services, which allow you reduce the amount of direct-mail marketing and telemarketing you receive from many national companies for five years.

When you register with these services, your name will be put in a "delete" file that is updated four times a year—in January, April, July, and October. The DMA makes this file available to direct-mail and telephone marketers. Two to three months after your name is entered into the quarterly file, you should notice a decrease in the number of solicitations you receive. However, your registration will not stop mailings or calls from organizations not registered with the DMA's Mail and Telephone Preference Services.

To have your name deleted from many direct-mail or telemarketing lists, write your own letter and mail it to:

For direct-mail marketing:
Direct Marketing Association
Mail Preference Service
PO Box 643
Carmel, NY 10512

For telemarketing:
Direct Marketing Association
Telephone Preference Service
PO Box 1559
Carmel, NY 10512

Web zone

Now choose one of the words or phrases to complete each sentence.

1. _____ mail is mail you did not ask to receive.
   Unsolicited / Solicited

2. Another way to say "reduce" is _____.
   cut down / delete

3. The DMA _____ the "delete" file four times a year.
   stops / updates

4. You need to _____ the DMA in order to have your name removed from
   write / call

   direct-mail and telemarketing lists.

5. You might still receive calls and mail from organizations not _____
   registered / decreased

   with the DMA Preference Services.

13 **Look at the Web site again. Then answer the questions.**

1. Which organization can help reduce the amount of direct mail marketing I get?

   _____

2. For how long will the amount of mail and calls I get be reduced?

   _____

3. When is the "delete" file updated?

   _____

4. Will registering with this service stop all unsolicited mail and calls?

   _____

5. How long does it usually take before I notice less mail and calls?

   _____

14 ▶ *CHALLENGE* **What's your advice? Read the questions. Then tell each person what to do. Use your own words and ideas.**

1. "I'd like my 15-year-old daughter to do volunteer work. Where are two places she could volunteer her time?"

   YOU _____

   _____

2. "I hate getting sales calls, but I don't want to be rude. What's the best way to respond to a telemarketing call?"

   YOU _____

   _____

3. "I'd like to help out at the bake sale next Saturday, but I'll be out of town. Is there anything else I could do to help?"

   YOU _____

   _____

15 Read the poster. Then check ☑ True or False.

Earth Day 2004

County Park Clean-Up Day

Let's work together to keep our country parks, pathways, and nature centers beautiful!

Volunteers needed for:

- Flower planting
- Trail clearing
- Cleaning
- Staining
- Graffiti removal
- Sweeping
- Pruning
- Painting

Sunday, April 25, 2004
9 a.m. to 3 p.m.
Rain or Shine
All ages welcome!

If you would rather make a cash contribution, please make your check payable to County Park Clean-Up.

Volunteers will receive valuable discount coupons redeemable at parks. Please dress appropriately for work (jeans, T-shirt, shorts, sneakers). All volunteers must wear gloves.

For more information log on to www.countyparkclean-up.com or call (914) 555-3874.

	True	False
1. This volunteer project is only for adults.	☐	☐
2. The volunteers will be cleaning and painting.	☐	☐
3. You can make a cash contribution to this cause.	☐	☐
4. The Clean-Up Day ends at 4:00 p.m.	☐	☐
5. Volunteers get paid for helping out.	☐	☐
6. Clean-Up Day will still go on even if it rains.	☐	☐

16 Answer these questions about County Park Clean-Up Day.

1. When is the County Park Clean-Up Day?

_____

2. What clothes should I wear?

_____

3. I'm going to be on vacation on County Clean-Up Day, but I'd still like to contribute. What can I do?

_____

4. Who do I make the check payable to?

_____

UNIT 2

Your environment

➤ Practical conversations

1 ➤ **VOCABULARY** Look at the pictures. What's the emergency? Write the sentence on the line.

1. _There's no heat._

2. _____

3. _____

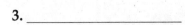

4. _____

5. _____

6. _____

2 Match the problem with the cause. Write the letter on the line.

1. I can't call you tonight. _____

2. Luka had to take a cold shower. _____

3. We can't watch our favorite TV show! _____

4. It's too hot to cook in our apartment. _____

5. I can close the door, but I can't lock it. _____

a. The cable is out.

b. There's no air conditioning.

c. The lock is broken.

d. There's no hot water.

e. My phone is out.

3 Complete the conversation. Use words from the box.

pipes	call	working	burst	give	water

A: How's it going, Arturo?

B: Not great. A pipe _____ on my street last night, and now there's
1.

no _____ in my apartment.
2.

A: That's terrible. Did you _____ the water company?
3.

B: Yes, two or three times. They're _____ on it.
4.

A: It was really cold last night. A lot of _____ burst.
5.

B: I know. Do you have water?

A: I think so. I'll _____ you a call when I get home.
6.

4 Have these problems ever happened to you? Check ☑ <u>yes</u> or <u>no</u>.

		yes	no
1.	A ball broke a window in your house / apartment.	❑	❑
2.	You called a plumber because a pipe burst.	❑	❑
3.	You lost power in your house / apartment.	❑	❑
4.	You talked to your building manager about a problem.	❑	❑
5.	You smelled gas in the kitchen.	❑	❑

5 Complete the conversation. Use your <u>own</u> words.

A: Manager's office. How may I help you?

B: Hi. This is _____ in apartment _____. I've got a problem.

A: What's wrong?

B: _____.

A: Well, I'm busy right now. Is it urgent?

B: _____.

A: OK. I'll _____.

➤ Practical grammar

6 **Complete each sentence with the present perfect or the simple past tense.**

1. We _____ the rental lease this morning.
   <u>sign</u>

2. They _____ the laundry room window yet.
   <u>not fix</u>

3. I _____ the landlord about the broken lock last week.
   <u>ask</u>

4. Saul still _____ an apartment that he likes.
   <u>not see</u>

5. _____ she already _____ the building manager?
   <u>call</u>

7 **Complete the paragraph about actions that started in the past with _for_ or _since_.**

My husband and I have lived in an apartment _____ eight years. We've
                                                          1.

paid the landlord more than $25,000 in rent _____ we moved in! But we have
                                                         2.

been saving $300 a month _____ the last four years and have been looking at
                                      3.

houses _____ April.
              4.

8 **Answer these questions about _yourself_. Use complete sentences.**

1. How long have you lived in the United States?

   _____

2. Where did you live before that?

   _____

3. How long have you been studying English?

   _____

9 ➤ *CHALLENGE* **Look at the information about Abou Bah. Complete the sentences about his life. Use the present perfect, the present perfect continuous, or the simple past tense. Use July 10 as today's date.**

	moved into a new apartment in Newton	hot weather started	air conditioner stopped working; called the building manager	called the building manager's office again	called the building manager's office again	visited the building manager's office
	June 10	July 1	July 5	July 7	July 8	July 9

1. Abou Bah _____ in Newton for _____.

2. The hot weather _____ on July 1.

3. The air conditioner _____ on July 5.

4. Mr. Bah _____ the building manager every day since July 5.

5. He _____ the building manager's office yesterday.

10 **Complete the sentences about <u>yourself</u>.**

1. I _____ since I moved here.

2. My family _____ for _____ years.

3. I have never _____.

➤ **Authentic practice**

11 **Read. Choose _your_ response. Fill in the ovals.**

1. "Have you had a chance to check on the outside light?"

    ⓐ No, I didn't.   ⓑ No, not yet.

2. "Any other questions about the lease?"

    ⓐ Yes. Is that a problem?   ⓑ Yes. Are utilities included?

3. "Can I get back to you on that?"

    ⓐ I hope not.   ⓑ Sure.

4. "Do you know the policy on pets?"

    ⓐ Not off the top of my head. I'll check.   ⓑ It's out again.

5. "Subletting is allowed for periods no longer than six months."

    ⓐ Do I need written approval?   ⓑ Any other questions?

12 **Read the conversation between a prospective tenant and a rental agent.**

Tenant: I've finished looking over the lease. Do you mind if I ask you a couple of questions?

Agent: Sure. Go ahead.

Tenant: It says here that utilities are included. What does that mean?

Agent: We pay the gas and electricity. The phone is your responsibility.

Tenant: What about cable TV?

Agent: You're responsible for that too.

Tenant: OK, fair enough. And what if there's an emergency?

Agent: What do you mean, "emergency"?

Tenant: Well, for example, if a pipe bursts or there's no heat. Who do I call?

Agent: Call the building supervisor. Her apartment is on the first floor.

What's their responsibility? Complete the chart.

Tenant	
Rental agent	
Building supervisor	

13 Complete the conversation. Use words from the box.

security	burst pipe	burners	dead-bolt
switches	leaks	electrical	circuit breakers

Sara: I'm going to see some apartments tomorrow. Do you have any advice for me?

Ryan: Well, I think _____ is very important. Make sure the front and
          1.

back doors have _____ locks on them.
                   2.

Sara: OK. What else?

Ryan: Look for _____ problems, like frayed wires, tripped
                   3.

_____, or missing _____.
        4.   5.

Sara: I hadn't thought of that. Is there anything else?

Ryan: Let's see . . . In the kitchen, be sure to turn on all the _____ on the
                                                                    6.

stove. I'd also check under all the sinks in the apartment for _____.
                                                              7.

You don't want to have to deal with a _____ once you move in.
                                       8.

Sara: Those are great tips. Thanks, Ryan!

14 What would you look for? Give two examples of what you would look for in a new house or
apartment for each of the categories. Use ideas from your Student's Book and your <u>own</u> ideas.

Security	
Fire code	
Pest infestation	
Appliances	
Plumbing	

15 **Read the information from the HUD Web site.**

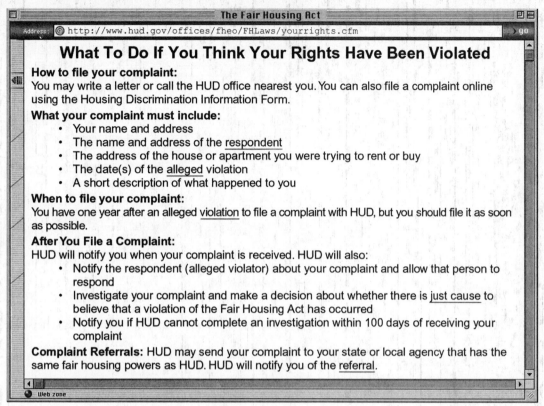

Now choose the correct answer. Circle the letter.

1. How much time after an alleged violation of your rights do you have to file a complaint?

   a. one year   **b.** 100 days

2. What must be included in your complaint?

   a. a copy of the lease   **b.** the alleged violator's name and address

3. Who may HUD refer your complaint to?

   a. the police   **b.** your state housing agency

16 **Look at the underlined words in the Web article. Match the underline word(s) with its meaning. Write the letter on the line.**

1. violation _____   **a.** an action that breaks the law

2. respondent _____   **b.** good reason

3. alleged _____   **c.** not proven

4. just cause _____   **d.** person your complaint is about

5. referral _____   **e.** something sent somewhere else

17 Read the Housing Discrimination Information form. Then check ☑ the information found on the form.

1. ☐ the landlord's phone number
2. ☐ Ms. Syed's phone number
3. ☐ the amount of rent for the apartment
4. ☐ the date of the alleged violation
5. ☐ the date the complaint was resolved
6. ☐ the address of the apartment

Housing Discrimination Information Form

YOUR NAME: _Sofia Syed_   PHONE: _(302) 555-8012_
YOUR ADDRESS: _14 Elm Rd_ CITY: _Hanover_ STATE: _DE_ ZIP CODE: _19802_

1. What happened to you? _I called about an apartment I saw advertised in the local paper. I left a message that I'd like to see it, but the landlord never called me back. I called again, but left a different name. The landlord called me back immediately to make an appointment to see the apartment._

2. Why do you think you were being discriminated against? _I believe that the landlord doesn't want to rent to an Indian._

3. Who do you believe discriminated against you?
   ☑ landlord/owner   ☐ banker
   ☐ real estate agent/compay   ☐ other: _____
   Name: _Eric Braxton_
   Address: _9640 Shaw Dr. Hanover, DE 19802_

4. Where did the alleged act of discrimination occur?
   ☐ at apartment/house   ☐ at bank
   ☑ on the phone   ☐ other: _____
   Address of apartment/house: _661 Fairhaven St. Easton, DE 19711_

5. When did the alleged discrimination occur? _11/10/03_

Signature _Sofia Syed_   Date _11/14/03_

18 Complete the sentences. Circle the letter.

1. _____ filed a housing discrimination complaint.
   a. Eric Braxton   b. Sofia Syed

2. The alleged violator is _____.
   a. Eric Braxton   b. Sofia Syed

3. The landlord called back _____.
   a. after Sofia's first call   b. after Sofia left a different name

4. The apartment she wanted to rent is at _____.
   a. 661 Fairhaven St.   b. 14 Elm Rd.

5. She thinks she was discriminated against because _____.
   a. of her nationality   b. she has young children

UNIT 3

Your equipment and machines

➤ Practical conversations

1 ➤ *VOCABULARY* **Look at the pictures. Fill in the blanks with words from the box.**

tailgate   not stopping   sideswiped   totaled   rear-ended   signal

1. Michael got a ticket for

   _____ at a stop sign.

3. Someone _____ my car
   when it was parked in the lot!

5. It's dangerous to _____
   on the highway at rush hour.

2. I need a new car. Mine was

   _____ yesterday.

4. We _____ another car
   this morning.

6. Why didn't you _____
   before making a turn?

2 ➤ *VOCABULARY* **Complete the sentences. Choose words. Write the words.**

1. It's important to _____ before you change lanes or make a turn.
   signal / tailgate

2. A _____ sign has eight sides.
   yield / stop

3. Using a _____ while you're driving can be dangerous.
   cell phone / license

4. When driving, you should always have your license and _____.
   registration / ticket

3 **Put the conversation in order. Write the number on the line.**

___1___ I had to take the bus today. My car is at the auto repair shop.

_____ That's good. Did you get a ticket?

_____ Why? Did you have an accident?

_____ No, thank goodness. It was just a fender bender.

_____ Oh, no! Were you hurt?

_____ Yes. I was turning right out of a parking lot, and another car hit me.

___7___ No, but the other driver did. He didn't stop at the stop sign.

4 **Complete the conversation. Use your own words.**

A: You look upset. Is there anything wrong?

B: Oh, I got a ticket today.

A: Really? What for?

B: For _____.

A: This has been a bad week for driving. My husband had an accident yesterday.

B: Oh, no! What happened?

A: _____.

B: Was anyone hurt?

A: _____.

B: And will the insurance cover the damage?

A: _____.

➤ Practical grammar

5 Complete the sentences with gerunds. Use the verbs from the box.

| break | see | use | ~~go~~ | observe | drive | stop | ask |

My brother got a ticket last week for _____*going*_____ through a red light. He was
                                        1.

driving home from work, and he was thinking about _____ his boss for a
                                                    2.

promotion. Instead of _____ the traffic light, he just kept _____ .
                       3.   4.

A few days later, he got a ticket in the mail for not _____ at a red light. He
                                                      5.

didn't remember _____ a police officer at the intersection. The ticket said
                 6.

that the city is now _____ red light cameras to catch drivers
                     7.

_____ the law. So be careful out there!
8.

6 Read Grace's date book for November 17. Then answer the questions with infinitives of purpose.

1. Why did Grace go to Speedy Auto Service?

_____

2. Why did she drive to the supermarket?

_____

3. Why did she call the doctor?

_____

4. Why did she go to the municipal courthouse?

_____

5. Why did she drive to the post office?

_____

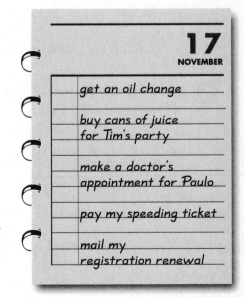

17
NOVEMBER

get an oil change

*buy cans of juice
for Tim's party*

*make a doctor's
appointment for Paulo*

pay my speeding ticket

*mail my
registration renewal*

7 Complete each sentence with a gerund or an infinitive of purpose.

1. Don't forget _____ when getting on the highway.
   to yield / yielding

2. You need to take a drug and alcohol class _____ a license.
   to get / for getting

3. _____ old enough to get a license doesn't always mean
   To be / Being

   that you're a good driver.

4. I got in trouble _____ my brother's car.
   to total / for totaling

5. Remember _____ before _____ lanes.
   to signal / signaling   _to change / changing_

6. It's important to pay more attention _____ than to
   to drive / to driving

   your passengers.

7. It's against the law _____ in a loading zone.
   to park / parking

8 ➤ CHALLENGE Look at the answer. Write a question.

1. _What did you get a ticket for?_ _____

   I got a ticket for not signaling.

2. _Why_ _____?

   I called the insurance company to report the accident.

3. _Why_ _____?

   She stopped to make a phone call.

4. _Why_ _____?

   Having a car is important for getting to work.

9 Complete the sentences. Use an infinitive of purpose or a gerund.

1. People often get tickets for _____.

2. Juan got a driver's license _____.

3. No matter who you are, there's no excuse for not _____.

➤ Authentic practice

10 **Read. Choose your response. Fill in the ovals.**

1. "I clocked you at 40 in a 25 zone."

   ⓐ What time is it?   ⓑ Was I really going that fast?

2. "Are you aware that your registration expired last month?"

   ⓐ Actually, no. I'm sorry.   ⓑ I left myself a little extra time.

3. "I'm going to have to ticket you for tailgating."

   ⓐ Thanks for letting me off easy.   ⓑ I'm sorry, officer. There's no excuse.

4. "You ran a red light back there."

   ⓐ I did? I'm sorry, I didn't realize that.   ⓑ No one got hurt.

5. "Next time you might not be so lucky."

   ⓐ I totaled the car.   ⓑ I know. You're right.

11 **Complete the conversation. Write the letter on the line.**

A: Have you ever been in an accident?

B: _____
       1.

A: Once, last year.

B: _____
       2.

A: I was just sitting in traffic and someone pulled out into me.

B: _____
       3.

A: No, I wasn't. It was just a fender bender. But I was very upset.

B: _____
       4.

A: Yes, they did. The officer wrote up an accident report.

B: _____
       5.

A: Yes, thank goodness. I didn't have to pay for anything.

a. Did your insurance cover the damage?

b. Of course. Did the police come?

c. No, I haven't. I've been lucky. What about you?

d. That's too bad. I hope you weren't hurt.

e. Really? What happened?

12 Read the brochure from the National Highway Traffic Safety Administration.

NHTSA

People Saving People
www.nhtsa.dot.gov.

AGGRESSIVE DRIVERS:

- Use their cars to take out their frustrations on anybody at any time.

- Run stop signs and red lights, speed, tailgate, weave in and out of traffic, pass on the right, make unsafe lane changes, make hand and facial gestures, scream, honk, and flash their lights.

- Drive too fast, change lanes too frequently and suddenly without signaling, pass on the shoulder, and may threaten—verbally or through gestures—motorists in front of them.

IF YOU ARE CONFRONTED BY AGGRESSIVE DRIVERS:

- Make every attempt to get out of their way. Do not challenge them by speeding up or trying to stay in your travel lane.

- Wear your seat belt. It will protect you in case you need to make a sudden driving maneuver, and it will protect you in a crash.

- Avoid making eye contact.

- Ignore gestures and refuse to return them.

- Report aggressive drivers to the appropriate authorities by providing a vehicle description, license number, location, and, if possible, direction of travel.

- If you have a cell phone, and can do it safely, call the police—many have a special number (e.g., 911 or #77).

Now check ☑ **T** (True), **F** (False), or **?** (I don't know).

	T	F	?
1. Aggressive driving is very dangerous.	☐	☐	☐
2. Most aggressive drivers are men.	☐	☐	☐
3. If an aggressive driver tailgates you, you should stay in your lane.	☐	☐	☐
4. You should look directly at the aggressive driver and gesture him or her to stop.	☐	☐	☐
5. If you can, you should report aggressive driving to the police.	☐	☐	☐
6. You should always use a cell phone right away to report aggressive driving.	☐	☐	☐

13 **What kind of driver does this? Write <u>good driver</u> or <u>aggressive driver</u> on the line.**

1. Runs red lights and stop signs.   <u>aggressive driver</u>

2. Uses a signal when making turns.   _____

3. Flashes headlights at slower-moving cars.   _____

4. Weaves in and out of traffic at high speed. _____

5. Yields to cars in the rotary.   _____

6. Observes the speed limit.   _____

7. Honks excessively.   _____

8. Makes hand gestures at other drivers.   _____

14 **What suggestions do you have for new drivers in your city or town? Write things new drivers should and should not do. Use your <u>own</u> words.**

<u>Things drivers should do</u>

1. *Use a signal when changing lanes.* _____

2. _____

3. _____

<u>Things drivers should avoid doing</u>

1. *Don't flash your lights at other cars.* _____

2. _____

3. _____

15 **Complete the chart. Put a check ☑ in the correct box.**

	OK	Not OK
1. Leaving an accident if you've damaged someone's property		
2. Stopping to help someone who is in real danger		
3. Calling 911 if you see someone in trouble		
4. Pretending to be a doctor to give medical help		
5. Treating others as you wish others would treat you		

16 **Read the sentences. Then choose the word or phrase that is closest in meaning to the underlined word(s). Circle the letter.**

1. I was <u>distracted</u> for a second when the baby threw down her bottle.

   a. angry   **b.** not paying attention   **c.** dangerous

2. It's against the law to <u>leave the scene of</u> an accident.

   a. go away from   **b.** leave without looking at   **c.** leave your car at

3. <u>Put yourself in the shoes of</u> the owner of the damaged car.

   a. Pay attention to   **b.** Describe the accident to   **c.** Think about the feelings of

4. There's nothing you can do now, but <u>let this be a lesson to you</u>.

   a. learn something from this   **b.** tell someone about this   **c.** ask someone about this

5. Pavlina told me that if I stop to help and something goes wrong, someone could <u>sue me</u>.

   a. give money to me   **b.** help me   **c.** take me to court for money

17 **Complete the sentences. Write the word(s) on the line.**

1. We have a _____ to help us look under the hood in the dark.

                 cell phone / flashlight

2. I just bought _____ in case my car battery dies.

              jumper cables / flares

3. It's really dark on this road. It's a good thing we have _____ to light.

                                        flares / maps

4. All cars come with a _____ and a _____.

                flashlight / jack   spare tire / blanket

5. If we had a _____, we wouldn't be lost right now!

       map / registration card

6. It's a good idea to carry a _____ with you so you can call 911

                license / cell phone

   in an emergency.

UNIT 4

Your customers

➤ Practical conversations

1 **➤ VOCABULARY** **Read the sentences. What does each person need? Match each sentence with a service or amenity. Write the letter on the line.**

1. I lost a button on my shirt. ____

2. My wife wants to iron her dress. ____

3. I want to use the swimming pool. ____

4. We want to eat breakfast in our room. ____

5. I'd like to have something to read in the morning. ____

6. I need 30 copies of this by tomorrow morning. ____

a. photocopies

b. a sewing kit

c. an ironing board

d. extra towels

e. room service

f. a newspaper

2 **Complete the conversation. Use words from the box.**

newspaper	brought	apology	pillows
use	Front desk	never	right

A: _____. How may I help you?
　　　　　1.

B: Hi. This is Ms. Sanchez in Room 212. I asked for some extra _____
　　　　　　　　　　　　　　　　　　　　　　　　　　　　　　　2.

an hour ago, and they _____ came.
　　　　　　　　　　3.

A: I'm sorry, Ms. Sanchez. I'll have them _____ up to you _____
　　　　　　　　　　　　　　　　　　　4.　　　　　　　　　5.

away. Is there anything else you need?

B: Well, I could _____ today's _____ if you have one.
　　　　　　　　　　6.　　　　　　　　7.

A: Of course. And please accept my _____.
　　　　　　　　　　　　　　　　　8.

3 Respond to these complaints and requests. Use <u>Right away</u> or <u>I'm so sorry</u>.

1. I'd like a newspaper, if you have an extra one. _____

2. There's no hot water in my room. _____

3. There's no one working in the gift shop. _____

4. I need directions to downtown. _____

5. The cable is out on the TV in my room. _____

6. I'd like to order room service. _____

4 Complete the conversation. Use the pictures and your <u>own</u> words.

A: Housekeeping.

B: Hi. This is _____ at the front desk. Would it be possible to take

_____ to Room _____ right away?

A: Of course. Is there anything else?

B: Yes. They'd also like _____.

A: Sure, no problem.

5 What's important to you at a hotel? Fill in the chart with your <u>own</u> ideas.

The hotel should have	The hotel doesn't need to have

➤ Practical grammar

6 Complete the paragraph with <u>some</u> or <u>any</u>.

Sam Markoff works in Housekeeping at the Old Colonial Hotel. At 8:30 this

evening, Mr. Benson, the guest in Room 328, called because there wasn't _____
1.

shampoo in his room. Sam took _____ up to him. When he arrived,
2.

Mr. Benson asked Sam for _____ extra coffee cups. Sam checked the
3.

Housekeeping closet, but there weren't _____. He found _____ in the
4.   5.

kitchen, and took them to the room. Then Mr. Benson had _____ questions
6.

about restaurants in the area. Sam didn't have _____ more time, so he gave
7.

Mr. Benson the names of _____ restaurants and then went to take care of
8.

_____ other requests.
9.

7 Write your <u>own</u> sentences. Use a word or phrase from each column.

| There is
There are
There isn't
There aren't | some
any | shampoo
meals
coffee
room service
water on the floor
guests
job openings
water glasses | in the conference room
on the eighth floor
in Room 516
on the third shelf
at the Good Night Motel
in the bathroom
on weekends
after 11 p.m. |

1. _*There isn't any coffee in the conference room.*_____

2. _____

3. _____

4. _____

5. _____

6. _____

8 ➤ *CHALLENGE* **Look at the answer. Then complete the question. Use <u>some</u> or <u>any</u>.**

1. **A:** *Do you want some* _____ more coffee?

   B: Yes, please. And I'd like some toast too.

2. **A:** _____ good movies on your vacation?

   B: Yes, we did. Actually, we saw three.

3. **A:** _____ clean towels in the supply room?

   B: No, there aren't. I'll get some from Housekeeping.

4. **A:** _____ phone calls from your room?

   B: No, we didn't. We didn't use the phone at all.

5. **A:** _____ help with paying the bills?

   B: Yes, thanks, I could. I have a lot of other things to do.

9 **Complete the sentences. Use your <u>own</u> words.**

1. I need some _____ because _____.

2. There are some _____ in our city.

3. There weren't any _____ here last year.

➤ Authentic practice

10 Read. Choose your response. Fill in the ovals.

1. "Would it be possible to get a rollaway bed?"

   ⓐ Is facing the parking lot OK?   ⓑ There's one still available.

2. "What time is check-out?"

   ⓐ At noon.   ⓑ It's $89 a night.

3. "I see you've requested a non-smoking room."

   ⓐ That's right.   ⓑ Here you go.

4. "I'd like to get an extra key card for the room."

   ⓐ Let me call the bellman for you.   ⓑ That's no problem at all.

5. "I need to be certain that the room isn't too noisy."

   ⓐ Let me know if it's not satisfactory.   ⓑ Are you checking in?

11 Who says this? Check ☑ hotel clerk or hotel guest.

	hotel clerk	hotel guest
1. "I have a reservation."	❑	❑
2. "Let me call the bellman for you."	❑	❑
3. "I see you'll be with us for two nights."	❑	❑
4. "I need to be certain that that's a non-smoking room."	❑	❑
5. "Are you checking in?"	❑	❑
6. "Do you have room service in this hotel?"	❑	❑
7. "Can I make an imprint of your credit card?"	❑	❑
8. "I'll need a wake-up call tomorrow morning."	❑	❑

12 Read the online hotel reservation form. Then complete the paragraph.

```
┌─────────────────────────────────────────────────────────────────────────┐
│ ▭▭▭▭▭▭▭▭         Skyview Suites Reservations         ▭▭▭▭▭▭▭ ▣▤│
│ Address: @ http://skyviewsuites                                    ⟩ go │
├─────────────────────────────────────────────────────────────────────────┤
│  Skyview Suites Conference Center              Reservations              │
│                                                                          │
│  Date of booking    February 1                                          │
│  Arrival date   February 8              Departure date   February 10    │
│  Occupancy [select one]   ○ 1 person   ○ 2 persons   ● more             │
│  Room type [select one]   ○ single     ● double      ○ suite            │
│  Beds [select one]        ○ king       ○ queen       ● two queens       │
│                                                                          │
│  Traveler contact information                                           │
│  Name      Edward Morgan                                                │
│  Address   3892 Buena Vista Dr.                                         │
│            Arlington, VA  22204                                         │
│                                                                          │
│  Payment information                                                    │
│  Credit card [select one]   ● USExpress   ○ MultiCard   ○ Wild Card     │
│  Card number  3984 4930 4721        Expiration date 7/31/06  Agent Hai  │
│  Reservation number  T290                                               │
└─────────────────────────────────────────────────────────────────────────┘
```

_____ made a reservation at the _____ Conference
　　　1.　　　　　　　　　　　　　　　　　　　　　　2.

Center on _____. He plans to arrive on _____ and stay for
　　　　　　3.　　　　　　　　　　　　　　　　　　　4.

_____ nights. He'll be traveling with his wife and two children.
　　5.

Mr. Morgan asked for a _____ room with two _____ beds.
　　　　　　　　　　　　　6.　　　　　　　　　　　　　7.

He guaranteed his reservation for a late arrival with his _____ credit card.
　　　　　　　　　　　　　　　　　　　　　　　　　　　　　8.

_____ took Mr. Morgan's call and made the reservation. Mr. Morgan's
　　9.

reservation number is _____.
　　　　　　　　　　　　　10.

30　　Unit 4

13 ➤ CHALLENGE **Look at the available rooms at the Skyview Suites.**

| Room 235 | Room 127 | Room 502 | Room 301 | Room 518 |

Which room would you recommend for each group of guests? Write the room number on the line. Use each room number only once.

1. Jean and Fred Cowan with their two young children   Room **502**

2. Mrs. Choi, with her husband, their two sons, and her mother   Room _____

3. Tsega Haile, traveling on business; needs a place to work
   in her room   Room _____

4. Luz Herrera and her friend, Asha Blair, attending a conference;
   need a place to keep and cook food in their room   Room _____

5. Nancy Davidoff and her eight-year-old son   Room _____

14 **Read the sentences. Then choose the word or phrase that is closest in meaning to the underlined word(s). Circle the letter.**

1. Your family's <u>tastes</u> are very important when planning a vacation.

   a. plans   **b.** reservations   **c.** likes and dislikes

2. It's possible to save a lot of money on cars, fares, and hotels if you <u>book</u> it in advance.

   a. reserve   **b.** travel   **c.** write

3. While some package deals are legitimate, don't <u>fall for</u> one that claims to be free.

   a. complain about   **b.** be tricked by   **c.** trip over

4. Pressuring you to send cash is a <u>red flag</u>.

   a. sign of trouble   **b.** good idea   **c.** real bargain

5. There's no such thing as <u>a free lunch</u>.

   a. getting food   **b.** saving money   **c.** getting something for
      without paying   nothing

15 Read the information about travel safety. Then answer the questions.

✈ Planning a vacation?
Get your money's worth with these tips from the **Federal Trade Commission**

▷ **Be wary!** Watch out for "bargain" vacation offers on postcards and certificates. Hidden charges can add up.

▷ **Don't be surprised.** Get the total cost in writing and know what it includes before you pay.

▷ **Protect yourself.** Give bank or credit card information only to businesses you know and trust. Never give unsolicited callers your bank account or credit card number.

▷ **Pay by credit card.** It gives you more protection than cash or a check. If you don't get what you paid for, you may be able to dispute the charges with your credit card

company.

▷ **Go with who you know.** Try to buy your vacation travel package from a business you know. If possible, deal with businesses that belong to professional associations. If you're not familiar with a company, get its complete name, address, and local telephone number.

▷ **Learn the vocabulary.** "You have been selected to receive our Dream Vacation offer" doesn't mean you'll get a free vacation. It means you'll be offered an opportunity to pay for a trip that may or may not be to your taste. "Subject to availability" means you may not get the accommodations you want when you want them. "Blackout periods" are blocks of dates (usually around holidays or peak season) when no discount travel is available.

1. Where are these travel tips from? _____

2. What should you do before you pay ? _____

3. Why is it safer to pay by credit card? _____

_____

4. What is a "blackout period"? _____

_____

16 Answer the questions about travel. Use ideas from your Student's Book and your <u>own</u> ideas.

1. "What does it mean to be 'cash smart'?"

   YOU _____

   _____

2. "I don't have access to the Internet. What are some other places where I can get information about good prices on travel?"

   YOU _____

   _____

3. "What are some things that could be included in a vacation package?"

   YOU _____

   _____

4. "What's the most important thing to do when planning a vacation?"

   YOU _____

   _____

UNIT 5

Your time

➤ Practical conversations

1 **➤VOCABULARY** Match each sentence and responses. Write the letter on the line.

1. These library books are overdue. ___
2. I forgot to register to vote again. ___
3. My driver's license expired last month. ___
4. We paid our credit card bill late again. ___
5. I tried to sign up for art class,
    but I missed the deadline. ___

a. You'll get a ticket.
b. You'll have to wait until next term.
c. You'll have to pay a fine.
d. You'll have to wait for the next election.
e. You'll have to pay a late fee and
    interest.

2 Complete the conversation. Use the words from the box.

| supposed | advice | wait | forgot | term |
| yesterday | deadline | register | believe | way |

A: When is the _____ to _____ for the customer service training?
                        1.   2.

B: Actually, it was _____. You missed it.
                        3.

A: Oh, no! I can't _____ it! I was _____ to register last week,
                        4.   5.

but I _____.
        6.

B: Guess you'll have to wait for next _____. Can I give you some
                                           7.

_____?
        8.

A: Sure.

B: Register early! That _____ you won't have to _____.
                              9.   10.

3 Complete the chart. Use ideas from your Student's Book and your <u>own</u> ideas.

Things you renew	Things you return	Things you register for
driver's license		

4 Look at the underlined words and phrases. Match each underlined word or phrase with its meaning in the sentence. Write the letter on the line.

1. You'll probably have to pay <u>a fine</u>. ___
2. I need to <u>reschedule</u>. ___
3. Are you going to <u>renew</u> your lease? ___
4. <u>That way</u> I won't forget it. ___
5. Oh, no! I <u>missed</u> Lee's birthday! ___
6. I <u>was supposed to</u> drop off my car, but I forgot. ___
7. All classes are full. You'll have to wait for the next <u>term</u>. ___

a. semester
b. planned to
c. extra money
d. arrange to continue
e. forgot
f. if I do that
g. make a new appointment

5 Complete the conversation. Use the pictures or your <u>own</u> words.

A: I don't believe it!

B: What's wrong?

A: Oh, I was supposed to _____

by _____ , but I forgot.

B: That's too bad. Now you'll have to _____. Maybe you

should _____. That way you won't forget again.

A: That's good advice. Thanks!

➤ Practical grammar

6 **Read the conditional sentences. Check ☑ the type of condition.**

	real condition	unreal condition
1. If you renew your library books today, you won't have to return them until next month.	❏	❏
2. If I were you, I'd register for classes today.	❏	❏
3. If you have to reschedule, we ask that you call 24 hours in advance.	❏	❏
4. You can check the due dates of your videos online if you have a computer.	❏	❏
5. I could register my car on my lunch break if it didn't take so long.	❏	❏
6. We'd remember more if we wrote it all down.	❏	❏
7. If I want to buy a house, I need to save money.	❏	❏
8. If my brother doesn't study, he'll fail the test.	❏	❏

7 **Read each real conditional sentence. Then rewrite the sentence as an unreal conditional.**

1. If I miss the deadline, I will be in big trouble.

   If I missed the deadline, I would be in big trouble.

2. Ivan helps me with my homework if he has time.

   _____

3. We won't pay late fees if we pay our bills on time.

   _____

4. If Sheila's computer skills improve, she will get a better job.

   _____

5. I ask my friends for help if I have too much on my plate.

   _____

8 ►*CHALLENGE* **Read the paragraph about Carolina.**

Carolina needs to renew her driver's permit. It expires tomorrow. She doesn't have enough time to practice driving, so she's not ready to take the driving test. Carolina's family doesn't have a car, so she has to ask friends to help her practice driving. She's worried about getting her permit renewed today, because she can't renew it after it expires. She'll have to take the permit test again.

Complete the real conditional sentences about Carolina.

1. Carolina wouldn't worry about renewing her permit *if she were able to renew it after it expires.*

2. Carolina won't pass the driving test _____

_____.

3. Carolina will have to take the permit test again _____

_____.

Complete the unreal conditional sentences about Carolina.

4. If Carolina had more time to practice driving, _____

_____.

5. If Carolina's family had a car, _____

_____.

6. If Carolina could renew her permit after it expired, _____

_____.

9 **Complete the sentences about <u>yourself</u>.**

1. If I could travel anywhere, _____

_____.

2. If I could have any job I wanted, _____

_____.

3. If I forget to register, _____

_____.

4. If I have overdue library books, _____

_____.

➤ Authentic practice

10 **Read. Choose your response. Fill in the ovals.**

1. "I'm juggling too many commitments right now."

   ⓐ Don't worry about it.   ⓑ Better late than never!

2. "Please accept my apology for missing the meeting."

   ⓐ I know you have a lot on your plate.   ⓑ How nice to see you.

3. "Can I offer you a little tip?"

   ⓐ That's good advice.   ⓑ Sure. What is it?

4. "Working two jobs is no picnic, is it?"

   ⓐ No, but I don't have much choice.   ⓑ I guess so.

5. "I'd make a list if I were in your shoes!"

   ⓐ You're right—I missed it.   ⓑ I'll start that tomorrow.

11 **Read the conversation. Then check ☑ T (True), F (False), or ? (I don't know).**

Nga: How do you keep track of everything you have to do?

Betty: Well, I'm actually not very good at it. I keep forgetting things I'm supposed to do.

Nga: Like what?

Betty: Well, like last week, I forgot a meeting I was supposed to go to.

Nga: That's a bad feeling.

Betty: Yes, it is. I make lists, but then I forget to look at them!

Nga: I know that if I didn't keep a date book, I'd miss things all the time.

Betty: Does your date book really help you?

Nga: It sure does. That way, all my obligations are in one place. I don't know how I ever managed without one.

Betty: Well, I'll have to try it. Thanks for the advice.

	T	F	?
1. Betty missed a meeting last week.	☐	☐	☐
2. Betty always remembers to check her lists.	☐	☐	☐
3. Nga uses a date book to remember commitments.	☐	☐	☐
4. Nga always remembers her appointments.	☐	☐	☐
5. Betty has been using a date book too.	☐	☐	☐

12 ➤**CHALLENGE**   Read the sentences. Is it <u>perfectionism</u>, <u>procrastination</u>, or <u>prioritization</u>? Write the word on the line.

1. I can return these books next week. I'll just pay the fine.   _procrastination_

2. If I can't do it well, I might as well not do it at all.   _____

3. First, I'll do the laundry. Then I'll go food shopping.   _____

4. This house is never clean enough!   _____

5. I always do the most important things before the least important things.   _____

13   Read Maria Rivera's to-do list. Then answer the questions.

To do!   Date: Thursday, July 15

Make a haircut appointment

Call Karen—dinner next week?

Drop off registration forms before 5:00!

Pick up dry cleaning

3:00—pick up kids

Mail medical insurance forms

Bake cookies for bake sale on Saturday

1. Which things does Ms. Rivera have to do today, no matter what? _____

_____

2. Which things can Ms. Rivera wait to do until tomorrow? _____

_____

3. Which things on the list can Ms. Rivera get someone else to do? _____

_____

14   Read the vehicle emissions inspection notice.

Vehicle Emissions Inspection Notice

State law requires that the vehicle listed below be brought for emissions testing between now and **March 6, 2004**

Vehicle Identifying Information:

LICENSE PLATE	VEHICLE ID	YEAR	MAKE	TITLE NO.
AR 498 T	BK1928375V983	87	Hurricane	398504

REGISTERED OWNER:
Moshe Lehr
116 Western Ave. Apt 4
Washington, DC 20014

This vehicle may be tested anytime after you receive this notice.

Vehicle Emissions Testing stations operate:
Mon - Fri: 8:00 AM-8:00 PM
Sat: 8:00 AM-12:00 PM

Most inspection stations are busiest between 10:00 AM and 2:00 PM on Monday, Tuesday, and Saturday .

Fees and payment
Inspection fee is $15.00. A late fee of $12.00 will be added the day after the due date. Cash, check, money order, traveler's check, and credit are acceptable.

If you are unable to bring your vehicle for testing by the due date, you may request an extension by calling (800) 555-3829. The extension must be requested before the due date listed above.

Name _____ ID _____ Date _____

Now complete the paragraph.

Mr. Lehr received this emissions testing notice on October 1, 2003. According to

the notice, Mr. Lehr must have his car emissions tested on or before _____.
1.

Mr. Lehr doesn't want to spend a lot of time waiting in line, so he'll try to go to the

station on _____, _____, or _____. If he goes before
2.   3.   4.

_____ or after _____, the inspection station won't be so busy.
5.   6.

The fee for the inspection is _____, unless Mr. Lehr misses the deadline.
7.

If he is one day late, he'll have to pay_____. If he wants an extension of the
8.

deadline, he would have to call before _____.
9.

15 **Find the examples of being late or missing a deadline in the letter from Deborah in Dallas.
Write the examples on the lines.**

Ask Joan

**Culture tips
fornewcomers**

Dear Joan:
I just can't get used to one thing in this country. I think people here are very nervous about time. And they are making me nervous too!

At work I have to punch a time clock, and if I'm five minutes late from my break, my manager gives me a dirty look. If I come late to someone's house for a party, they are unfriendly to me.

I think this is silly, and I think people should just relax! What would happen if someone brought a book back to the library a couple of days late? What would the big deal be? Sometimes it takes a little longer to finish the book. And if the people who are giving the party are my friends, why do they mind if I'm not right on time? And what's so terrible if I pay my rent a day or two late? The landlord has a lot of money. Believe me, he won't starve!

Please explain to me, Joan: Why are the people here so crazy about schedules and time? I think it's very unfriendly.

Deborah in Dallas

1. *coming back five minutes late from her break*

2. _____

3. _____

4. _____

16 Complete the sentences in the questionnaire. Use the words from the box.

| return | list | plate | calendar | starts | deadlines | expires | miss |

Is Time on Your Side?

How well are you juggling your time?
Take this quiz and find out!

Choose the answer that's closest to your style. Be truthful!

1. Your work _____ at 8:00 a.m. What time do you arrive at work?
   a. 7:50 a.m.   **b.** 8:00 a.m.   **c.** 8:05 a.m.

2. Your driver's license _____ on May 2. When do you renew it?
   a. April 3   **b.** April 30   **c.** May 2

3. You're having a party on Saturday night. When do you start cleaning your house?
   a. Thursday   **b.** Friday   **c.** Saturday afternoon

4. How often do you use a _____ to keep track of your commitments?
   a. always   **b.** sometimes   **c.** never

5. Your library books are due Tuesday. When do you _____ them?
   a. before Tuesday   **b.** Tuesday   **c.** after Tuesday

6. How do you feel about _____ ?
   a. They're helpful.   **b.** They're OK.   **c.** I hate them!

7. How often do you forget or _____ appointments?
   a. never   **b.** sometimes   **c.** often

8. When was the last time you made and checked a to-do _____ ?
   a. today   **b.** last week   **c.** I can't remember.

9. How good are you at prioritizing when you have a lot on your _____ ?
   a. great   **b.** usually OK   **c.** What does prioritize mean?

10. How would you describe your relationship with time?
    a. I've got plenty of it!   **b.** I could use some help.   **c.** I'm on total overload!

What's your time score? Count up your answers!

If you have mostly **a** answers:
Congratulations—you are the master of your time! Keep up the good work!

If you have mostly **b** answers:
You could use a little help managing your time. Know when to say no—and when to ask for help!

If you have mostly **c** answers:
You are an expert at procrastinating! Your motto: Better late than never. Start that To-Do list today, and work on those prioritization skills!

17 Now complete the questionnaire for <u>yourself</u> and check your score.

UNIT 6

Your supplies and resources

➤ Practical conversations

1 ➤ **VOCABULARY** Look at the pictures. Check ☑ <u>yes</u> or <u>no</u>.

1. construction

❑ yes ❑ no

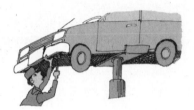

2. an auto repair

❑ yes ❑ no

3. plumbing

❑ yes ❑ no

4. dental work

❑ yes ❑ no

5. electrical work

❑ yes ❑ no

6. a paint job

❑ yes ❑ no

2 Should you get an estimate? Read the situations. Then write <u>yes</u> or <u>no</u>.

1. Fixing a broken pipe in your basement   _____

2. Getting a tree removed from your property   _____

3. Renewing a driver's license   _____

4. Taking books out of the library   _____

5. Buying a new shirt at the store   _____

6. Having your roof repaired   _____

3 Complete the conversation. Write the letter on the line.

A: I'd like to have my car painted.
Can you give me an estimate?

B: _____
   1.

A: It's a 2002 Monsoon SUV.

B: _____
   2.

A: How long do you think it'll take?

B: _____
   3.

A: That's not too bad. Can you put that in writing?

B: _____
   4.

a. About two days.

b. Monsoon SUV. . . OK.
   It'll be about $400.

c. Of course! I'll write it up
   for you now.

d. What kind of car is it?

4 ►**VOCABULARY** Complete the sentences. Write the missing letters on the lines.

1. The prices at Atlas Fencing are very r __ __ __ __ __ __ __ __ e .

2. My last mechanic always lied to me. Is yours h __ __ __ __ t ?

3. I need this pipe fixed right away. Can you do it f __ __ t ?

4. M & B Construction did a great job. I highly r __ __ __ __ __ __ __ __ d them.

5. She wouldn't give me an e __ __ __ __ __ __ __ e , so I called another company.

6. Our electrician is very e __ __ __ __ __ __ __ __ t . He doesn't waste any time.

5 Complete the conversation. Use your <u>own</u> words.

A: I'm looking for a good _____. Can you recommend anyone?

B: Well actually, I can. _____ name is _____.

A: Is _____ _____?

B: Yes. And _____ is very _____.

A: _____. I'll give _____ a call. Thanks.

42   Unit 6

➤ Practical grammar

6 **For each sentence, circle the subject and underline the verb.**

1. (We) got it in writing.

2. They wasted a lot of time.

3. The work took longer than we thought.

4. Those mechanics were reasonable, but not very fast.

5. I volunteered to help.

6. Pete's Plumbing does a really good job.

7. New construction is too expensive!

7 **Put the words in order. Write sentences or questions. Use correct capitalization and punctuation.**

1. tomorrow / the / estimate / they'll / bring / morning

   They'll bring the estimate tomorrow morning.

2. or / hours / the / will / take / eight / job / seven

   _____

3. needs / good / Ms. Lopez / electrician / a

   _____

4. insurance / cover / think / repairs / the / will / we / the

   _____

5. to / references / you / like / you / give / me / would / some

   _____

6. take / the / long / will / how / auto repair

   _____

8 **Rewrite the paragraphs with correct capitalization and punctuation.**

1. my daughter edith is eight years old she's in the third grade her school is on martin luther king drive her teacher's name is miss tam

    _____

    _____

    _____

2. we've lived in st louis for three years our doctor's name is dr cherala her office is in greenville she's the best doctor in missouri

    _____

    _____

    _____

9 ➤*CHALLENGE* **Address this envelope to a service provider you have used (for example: a doctor, a hairdresser, a mover). Use your name and address as the return address.**

➤ Authentic practice

🔟 Read. Choose your response. Fill in the ovals.

1. "Is the damage to the roof covered?"

   ⓐ Incredible.   ⓑ Absolutely.

2. "The thunderstorm was horrible. We're lucky no one got hurt."

   ⓐ Will you put that in writing?   ⓑ You can say that again.

3. "There's water damage in our bedroom. Are we insured for that?"

   ⓐ Check the policy.   ⓑ Ask around.

4. "Can you recommend someone to repair my windows?"

   ⓐ Personally, no.   ⓑ It'll be about $300.

5. "I think we should get another quote before we make a decision."

   ⓐ That's a relief.   ⓑ That's a good idea.

⓫ Complete the conversation. Use words from the box.

battery	towed	add	cover	broke down
policy	coverage	flat tire	auto	locked

Tom: What a month I'm having. Last week my car _____ and I had to have
                                                    1.

it _____. Then this morning I _____ my keys in the car. It's
        2.   3.

starting to run into a lot of money!

Suni: Don't you have roadside assistance _____?
                                                    4.

Tom: Roadside assistance? What's that?

Suni: It's a service you can _____ to your _____ insurance for
                                          5.   6.

only $12 a year.

Tom: Really? What does it _____?
                                        7.

Suni: Towing, lock outs, and _____ service. They'll even send some out to
                                          8.

help jump start your car if the _____ dies.
                                        9.

Tom: I'd better check my _____ to see if I have roadside assistance.
                                    10.

12 **Read the estimates. Then answer the questions.**

Odessa Painting
Boris Chertov, prop.

Paint three rooms, 2 coats
Three painters, $500 + tip
Start: Tuesday
Finish: Thursday

Velela Household Painting
15678 E. Dakota Avenue, Denver, CO 80232
(303) 555-7838

Paint three rooms, 2 coats
Two painters, $425 includes tip
Start: Monday
Finish: Thursday

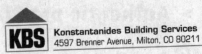

KBS Konstantanides Building Services
4597 Brenner Avenue, Milton, CO 80211

Paint three rooms, 2 coats
Four painters, $525 + tip and supplies
Start: Wednesday
Finish: Thursday

1. Who gave the most expensive estimate? _____

2. Which company can start the earliest? _____

3. Which company can do the job the fastest? _____

4. How much would the total cost be if you chose Odessa Painting and gave each

    painter a $10 tip? _____

5. Which company would you choose? Why? _____

    _____

13 **Read the article on insurance.**

Today's Life Magazine   November 2004 **41**

Insurance Basics
**How to protect your property, your resources, and your loved ones
Hope for the best. . . BUT plan for the worst**

Homeowner's Insurance
Your home is your most expensive <u>asset</u>, your shelter, and the place
you keep your belongings. Homeowner's insurance provides financial
protection against disasters—damage to your property and <u>injury</u> to
other people or their property. If you own a house or an apartment,
you need it.

Auto Insurance
Auto insurance protects you against financial loss if you have an
accident. It <u>generally</u> covers damage to or loss of your car and injury
or property damage to others. Most states require you to <u>carry</u> some
car insurance coverage.

Life Insurance
Life insurance pays your beneficiaries in case of your death. If other
people depend on your income, then you need life insurance. Life
insurance helps pay <u>short-term expenses</u>, such as funeral costs,
medical bills, debt, and taxes, and long-term expenses, such as college
expenses, mortgage payments, etc.

Key Insurance Terms

insurance A contract
between you and an
insurance company to
make payments to you or
another person in case of
injury, damage, or death

premium The amount
you pay the insurance
company for coverage

liability Your legal
responsibility to pay the
victim of injury or
damage you cause either
directly or indirectly

beneficiary A person
who receives payments
from an insurance
company

claim A report you
make to an insurance
company in order to
receive payments you
are entitled to under the
terms of your policy

Now look at the underlined words in the article. Which words below are closest in meaning to the underlined words? Write the word on the line.

1. have *carry*
2. things you own _____
3. money you spend immediately _____
4. physical harm _____
5. usually _____

14 Choose the correct answer. Circle the letter.

1. The money you must pay if you are responsible for damage or an injury is your ____.

   a. insurance
   b. liability
   c. premium
   d. beneficiary

2. Homeowner's insurance protects your ____.

   a. assets
   b. medical bills
   c. cars
   d. college expenses

3. One type of insurance which you may be required by law to have is ____.

   a. life insurance
   b. health insurance
   c. auto insurance
   d. prescription insurance

4. Life insurance can help cover ____.

   a. property damage only
   b. property damage and short-term expenses
   c. short-term expenses only
   d. short-term and long-term expenses

15 Complete the sentences about yourself.

1. I _____ auto insurance because _____
   need / don't need
   _____.

2. I _____ homeowner's insurance because _____
   need / don't need
   _____.

3. I _____ life insurance because _____
   need / don't need
   _____.

16 **Read the information about lowering insurance costs.**

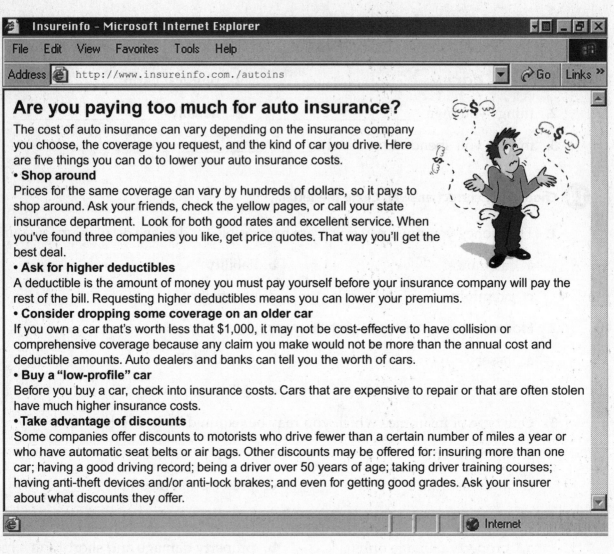

Insureinfo – Microsoft Internet Explorer

File   Edit   View   Favorites   Tools   Help

Address ▸ http://www.insureinfo.com./autoins ▾ ⟳ Go   Links »

Are you paying too much for auto insurance?

The cost of auto insurance can vary depending on the insurance company you choose, the coverage you request, and the kind of car you drive. Here are five things you can do to lower your auto insurance costs.

• Shop around

Prices for the same coverage can vary by hundreds of dollars, so it pays to shop around. Ask your friends, check the yellow pages, or call your state insurance department. Look for both good rates and excellent service. When you've found three companies you like, get price quotes. That way you'll get the best deal.

• Ask for higher deductibles

A deductible is the amount of money you must pay yourself before your insurance company will pay the rest of the bill. Requesting higher deductibles means you can lower your premiums.

• Consider dropping some coverage on an older car

If you own a car that's worth less that $1,000, it may not be cost-effective to have collision or comprehensive coverage because any claim you make would not be more than the annual cost and deductible amounts. Auto dealers and banks can tell you the worth of cars.

• Buy a "low-profile" car

Before you buy a car, check into insurance costs. Cars that are expensive to repair or that are often stolen have much higher insurance costs.

• Take advantage of discounts

Some companies offer discounts to motorists who drive fewer than a certain number of miles a year or who have automatic seat belts or air bags. Other discounts may be offered for: insuring more than one car; having a good driving record; being a driver over 50 years of age; taking driver training courses; having anti-theft devices and/or anti-lock brakes; and even for getting good grades. Ask your insurer about what discounts they offer.

🌐 Internet

Now complete the sentences. Write the words on the line.

1. When shopping around for auto insurance, be sure to look for _____
    and _____ .

2. You can lower your insurance premiums by asking for a _____ .

3. You should drop collision and comprehensive coverage if your car is
    _____ .

4. Cars that get stolen often or are expensive to repair are not _____
    cars.

5. If you have a car alarm and automatic seat belts, you may be able to get a
    _____ on your auto insurance.

UNIT 7

Your relationships

➤ Practical conversations

1 **➤VOCABULARY** **Are these opinions pro or con? Fill in the ovals.**

Capital punishment

Pro Con

1. I think taking a life is wrong.

2. It's too dangerous. An innocent person could be killed.

3. I believe it makes criminals think twice before they act.

Government censorship of books and movies

4. I should be able to see and read what I want.

5. I think criminals might copy violence they see in a movie.

Organized prayer in public schools

6. My children's religion is my business, not the schools'.

7. Prayer would make students behave better.

8. Prayer is religion, and religion doesn't belong in a public school.

2 **Complete the conversation. Use words from the box.**

| favor guess opinion matter think wrong against circumstances |

A: What do you _____ about having soda machines in schools?
1.

B: Actually, I'm _____ it.
2.

A: Really? Why?

B: Well, I think it's _____ for children to spend money on soda. And it's
3.

very unhealthy. What's your _____?
4.

A: I'm in _____ of it. Schools can make a lot of money from the machines.
5.

B: I _____ that's true. And under some _____ I think
6.   7.

they're OK. But not in an elementary school, no _____ what!
8.

3 Read the list of rules from different places. Do you agree or disagree with the rules?
Check ☑ your opinion.

	I agree	I disagree
1. You can't smoke in a school building.	❑	❑
2. Everyone in a car must wear a seat belt.	❑	❑
3. Small children must be in safety seats in a car.	❑	❑
4. People under 21 may not buy alcohol.	❑	❑
5. People under 18 may not buy cigarettes.	❑	❑
6. Motorcycle riders must wear a helmet.	❑	❑
7. Smoking is not allowed in restaurants.	❑	❑
8. You must have a license to own a gun.	❑	❑
9. You can't eat or drink in the library.	❑	❑
10. You must wear shoes and a shirt in a restaurant.	❑	❑

4 Complete the conversations. Use your own words.

1. **A:** There are just too many rules these days!

   B: What do you mean?

   A: Well, did you know that _____?

   B: Yes, I did. I'm in favor of it, because _____.

   A: I guess you have a point.

2. **A:** What's your opinion about _____?

   B: Well, I _____. What do you think?

   A: Actually, I'm _____ it. I believe _____.

   B: _____.

➤ Practical grammar

5 Write quotation marks and a period or a question mark at the end of the quoted speech.

1. Asha asked, Does this restaurant have a non-smoking section

2. The waitress answered, Yes. It's in the back

3. Danielle said, I thought all restaurants were entirely nonsmoking now

4. The waitress said, Maybe in some states, but not here

5. Asha asked, Would you rather eat somewhere else

6. Danielle replied, No, this is fine

6 Rewrite these sentences with correct punctuation and capitalization. Use commas, periods, question marks, and quotation marks.

1. Luis said did you know you have to wear a helmet when you ride your bicycle

   Luis said, "Did you know you have to wear a helmet when you ride your bicycle?"

2. Marcela said I thought that law was only for children

   _____

3. Luis responded no, it's for everyone

   _____

4. Marcela asked where can I get a helmet

   _____

5. Luis answered they're on sale at the bike store in Old Town

   _____

6. Marcela said thanks. I'll get one tomorrow

   _____

7 **Report what each person says.**

1. Jerry: I'm in favor of it.

   Jerry says he's in favor of it.

2. Lia: It's ridiculous that we can't smoke in the building.

   _____

3. Mr. Tan: I'm against prayer in schools.

   _____

4. Yuri: I believe that censorship is necessary.

   _____

5. Sophia: There are way too many rules.

   _____

6. Arturo: I disagree with that law.

   _____

7. Maria: It's wrong to take more than you can eat at a buffett.

   _____

8. Ava: I heard about that on the news.

   _____

8 **Answer the questions about <u>yourself</u>. Use indirect speech.**

1. What does your family say about you?

   _____

2. What do people in your home country say about the United States?

   _____

3. What do your classmates say about your school?

   _____

➤ Authentic practice

9 **Read. Choose your response. Fill in the ovals.**

1. "How about La Luna for lunch?"

   ⓐ It's a little pricey for me.   ⓑ Do you have a receipt?

2. "Do you have exact change?"

   ⓐ Sorry. It's out of my price range.   ⓑ Sure. Here you go.

3. "Just my luck. The gift-wrap desk is closed."

   ⓐ That's OK. It too expensive anyway.   ⓑ I'm against it.

4. "What do you think of this shirt?"

   ⓐ It's wrong no matter what.   ⓑ It's beautiful.

5. "What do you think of lowering the driving age to 15?"

   ⓐ I think I'll pass.   ⓑ I think it's ridiculous.

10 **Put the conversation in order. Write the number on the line.**

___1___ I think the Internet is a dangerous thing.

_____ Parental control software? What's that?

_____ There are a lot of things on it that children shouldn't see.

_____ Dangerous? Why?

_____ It's software that allows parents to restrict what children can see on the Web.

_____ That's a great idea. But I still think there should be limits to the Internet.

_____ True. But that's why there is parental control software.

_____ But that would be censorship. Are you in favor of that?

___9___ Hmmm. . . I'll have to think about that.

11 **Complete the conversation. Write the letter on the line.**

A: Did you hear what happened to Yusef?

B: _____
      1.

A: He was arrested yesterday for shoplifting.

B: _____
      2.

A: The Metro Mall. They say he stole a watch.

B: _____
      3.

A: I know. I'm sure he didn't do it.

B: _____
      4.

A: Yes. Ms. Wolf is his lawyer. She's very good.

B: _____
      5.

a. Does he have a lawyer?

b. No, I didn't. What?

c. I'm sure she'll prove he's innocent.

d. That's ridiculous. He's such a good kid.

e. Shoplifting? I don't believe it! From where?

12 **Read the advice from a civil liberties Web site. Fill in the missing words.**

witnesses	innocent	complain	argument	against
badge	calm		lawyer	touch

In Case of an Arrest

Address: @ http://yourrights.org   › go

In case of an arrest

1. Be polite and respectful. Never bad-mouth a police officer. Don't get into an
   _____.

2. Stay _____ and in control of your words, body language, and emotions.

3. Remember, anything you say or do can be used _____ you.

4. Keep your hands where the police can see them. Don't _____ any police officer.

5. Don't run. Don't resist even if you believe you are_____ .

6. Don't _____ on the scene or tell police they're wrong or say you're going to file a complaint.

7. Don't make statements about the incident. Ask for a _____ immediately upon your arrest.

8. Remember officers' _____ and patrol car numbers. Write down everything you remember ASAP.

9. Try to find _____ and their names and phone numbers.

Web zone

---

13 **Read the amendments from the Bill of Rights.**

Amendment I

Congress shall make no law respecting an establishment of religion, or prohibiting the free exercise thereof; or abridging the freedom of speech, or of the press; or the right of the people peaceably to assemble, and to petition the Government for a redress of grievances.

Amendment IV

The right of the people to be secure in their persons, houses, papers, and effects, against unreasonable searches and seizures, shall not be violated, and no Warrants shall issue, but upon probable cause, supported by Oath or affirmation, and particularly describing the place to be searched, and the persons or things to be seized.

Amendment VI

In all criminal prosecutions, the accused shall enjoy the right to a speedy and public trial, by an impartial jury of the State and district wherein the crime shall have been committed, which district shall have been previously ascertained by law, and to be informed of the nature and cause of the accusation; to be confronted with the witnesses against him; to have compulsory process for obtaining witnesses in his favor, and to have the Assistance of Counsel for his defence.

Amendment VII

In suits at common law, where the value in controversy shall exceed twenty dollars, the right of trial by jury shall be preserved, and no fact tried by a jury, shall be otherwise reexamined in any Court of the United States, than according to the rules of the common law.

44 *Our United States History*

Our United States History 45

Now look at the statements about rights below. Write the number of the amendment that applies to each statement.

1. The government may not tell people what religion to belong to. _____

2. The government may not search people's homes, papers, or property without a good reason. _____

3. The people have a right to a free press (newspapers, books, etc.). _____

4. A person who is accused of a crime has the right to see and hear from the witnesses against him or her. _____

5. A person who is accused of a crime has the right to a lawyer. _____

6. If the amount in question is more than $20, the alleged criminal has the right to a jury trial. _____

14 ▶ *CHALLENGE* **Look at the picture. Then fill in the blanks. Use the words from the box.**

witness	flag	state's attorney	jury box	defense attorney
robes	defendant	judge	jurors	witness stand

1. *jurors*
2. _____
3. _____
4. _____

5. _____
6. _____

7. _____
8. _____

9. _____

15 **Answer these questions about <u>yourself</u>.**

1. What rule from your job, school, or community do you agree with? Why?

   _____

   _____

2. What rule from your job, school, or community do you disagree with? Why?

   _____

   _____

UNIT 8

Your health and safety

➤ Practical conversations

1 Complete the conversation. Use words from the box.

fatty	report	limit	weight
cholesterol	milkshake	too	overweight

A: What's wrong?

B: I just got my medical _____ from my doctor.
                                    1.

A: Oh, really? What did it say?

B: It said that I'm a little _____ and that my _____ is
                                    2.   3.

   too high.

A: That's _____ bad. What do you have to do?
                    4.

B: The doctor says I have to stay away from _____ foods and watch
                                                        5.

   my _____.
            6.

A: Will that take care of it?

B: I hope so. Guess I shouldn't have had that _____ with lunch! I guess
                                                          7.

   I have to learn to _____ the amount and kinds of food I eat from now on.
                            8.

2 Think about these health problems. What should and shouldn't they do? List as many foods and activities as you can.

	should	shouldn't
People who are overweight		
People with high blood pressure		
People who have high cholesterol		

3 ▶ VOCABULARY **Complete the sentences. Write the missing letters on the lines.**

1. Janice has really bad m _ _ _ _ _ _ _ e headaches.

2. Aspirin may help you feel better, but it's not a c _ _ _ e.

3. Do you know of a good r _ _ _ _ _ y for a toothache?

4. You can get this diet pill without a p _ _ _ _ _ _ _ _ _ _ _ n.

5. I have to l _ _ _ _ t my salt because of my blood pressure.

6. If you have high c _ _ _ _ _ _ _ _ _ _ _ _ l you should stay away

   from fatty foods.

4 **Complete the conversations. Use your own words.**

1. **A:** What do you take when you have _____?

   B: I usually use _____.

   A: Does it help?

   B: _____.

2. **A:** Do you know of anything that cures _____?

   B: They say _____ can help.

   A: Where did you hear that?

   B: _____.

   A: OK. I guess it couldn't hurt to give it a try.

➤ Practical grammar

5 Write a sentence with <u>should have</u> or <u>shouldn't have</u> and a past participle to express regret.

1. I bought the big box of cookies.

   I shouldn't have bought the big box of cookies.

2. Luisa didn't ask her doctor to call her prescription in to the pharmacy.

   _____

3. The Olsons tried to move a heavy bookcase themselves.

   _____

4. Hanna gave her sister some of her prescription medicine.

   _____

5. Alain didn't ask his doctor to check his cholesterol.

   _____

6. I didn't start this exercise plan a long time ago.

   _____

6 Write sentences. Use a word or group of words from each column.

| I
She
He
We
You
They | should have
shouldn't have | bought
asked
tried
believed
chosen
stopped
checked with
eaten
written down
taken | exercising
that restaurant
your advice
that ad
that double cheeseburger
after 8:00
a doctor
the pharmacist
green tea
those salty chips
my mother's remedy |

1. _They should have checked with a doctor._

2. _____

3. _____

4. _____

5. _____

7 Complete each negative yes-no question.

1. _____ a prescription for that?
   you / need

2. _____ bad for you?
   smoking / be

3. _____ a lot of weight a few years ago?
   Mehmet / lose

4. _____ really expensive?
   health clubs / are

5. _____ that miracle diet drug?
   you / buy

8 Convert each sentence to a negative question.

1. I think you ordered a decaf coffee.

   Didn't you order a decaf coffee?

2. I think Maya had a check-up last week.

   _____

3. I think Linda looks wonderful!

   _____

4. I think you are taking medicine for your cholesterol.

   _____

5. I think you tried the same diet last year.

   _____

6. I think Eric is a volunteer paramedic.

   _____

7. I think Leon stopped smoking.

   _____

➤ Authentic practice

9 **Read. Choose <u>your</u> response. Fill in the ovals.**

1. "It says it's just as good for you as eating vegetables!"

    ⓐ Take my word for it.   ⓑ Don't be so gullible.

2. "Don't you like chocolate?"

    ⓐ Are you kidding? I can't pass it up.   ⓑ Of course I did.

3. "Look at this video: *Exercise for Couch Potatoes!*"

    ⓐ That's too bad.   ⓑ It couldn't hurt to give it a try.

4. "You know what they say. There's no free lunch."

    ⓐ I shouldn't have eaten that.   ⓑ You're right.

5. "Come on! You don't even know what's in it!"

    ⓐ The label says it's all natural.   ⓑ Maybe you could get your money back.

10 **Complete the conversation. Write the letter on the line.**

Val: I heard about a new herbal tea on TV the other night.

Alema: _____
⠀⠀⠀⠀⠀⠀1.

Val: Migraines. Don't you get those?

Alema: _____
⠀⠀⠀⠀⠀⠀2.

Val: So what do you do for them?

Alema: _____
⠀⠀⠀⠀⠀⠀3.

Val: The first thing to do is to find out if the remedy is even safe.

Alema: _____
⠀⠀⠀⠀⠀⠀4.

Val: Well, it couldn't hurt to ask your doctor about it.

Alema: _____
⠀⠀⠀⠀⠀⠀5.

Val   Alema

a. You're right. I'll ask about it at my next appointment.

b. I sure do. They're really painful.

c. What's it supposed to be good for?

d. I've tried prescription medicines and cutting down on caffeine, but nothing really helps.

e. Definitely. It has to be safe and not just a waste of my money.

11 **Look at the conversation again. Then complete the sentences. Use words from the box.**

suggests	limiting	headaches	gullible	safe	remedy

1. Val saw an ad for an herbal _____ on TV.

2. Val _____ herbal tea for Alema's migraines.

3. Alema has tried _____ caffeine, but it hasn't helped.

4. Alema doesn't want to be _____, so she's going to talk to her doctor first.

5. Val tells Alema to ask her doctor if the herbal tea is _____.

6. Migraines are very painful _____.

12 **Read the calorie chart and activities list.**

Carbonated sodas (per 1 cup)
Cola-type.. 95 calories
Fruit flavored ....115 calories

Juices (per 1/2 cup)
Apple juice, canned .... 60 calories
Grape juice, bottled .... 80 calories
Orange juice, canned............... 55 calories
Tomato juice .... 25 calories

Coffee and tea
Coffee, black .... 3–5 calories
with 1 tsp. sugar.................18–20 calories
with 1 tsp. cream.............. 13–15 calories
Tea, plain .... 0–1 calories
with 1 tsp. sugar................. 15–16 calories

Candy (per ounce)
Hard candy................................110 calories
Jelly beans................................105 calories
Marshmallows ....90 calories

Salty snacks
Corn chips (1 cup)............... 230 calories
Potato chips (1 cup) .... 115 calories
Stick pretzels (5) .... 10 calories
Air popcorn, no butter............. 25 calories
Peanuts (2 tablespoons)...... 105 calories

Cheese (per ounce)
American, processed............. 105 calories
Cottage, low-fat (2%) .... 25 calories

Fruits (raw)
Apple, 1 medium...................... 80 calories
Apricots, dried, 5 halves.......... 40 calories
Banana, 1 medium................ 105 calories
Dates, dried, 3 .... 70 calories
Grapes, 20................................... 30 calories
Orange, 1 medium .... 60 calories

Vegetables (raw)
Carrots, 1/2 cup grated........... 35 calories
Celery, 5-inch stalks, 3............. 10 calories
Pickle, 1 .... 15–20 calories

This chart shows the number of calories burned per hour by a 150-pound (68kg) person engaged in various activities.

Activity	Cal / hr	Activity	Cal / hr
Sitting quietly	84	Swimming (crawl, 20 yds/min)	288
Lying down or sleeping	90	Ice skating (9 mph)	384
Sitting and writing, talking, etc.	114	Scrubbing floors	440
Bicycling (5 mph)	174	Basketball (recreational)	450
Walking (2 mph)	198	Aerobic dancing	546
Dancing (ballroom)	210	Bicycling (13 mph)	612
Light housework, cleaning, etc.	246	Jogging (6 mph)	654
Volleyball (recreational)	264	Circuit weight training	756

Now choose the correct answer. Circle the letter.

1. Which food has the most calories?

   a. 20 grapes   **b.** 1/2 cup of tomato juice   **c.** 5 pretzel sticks

2. About how many calories are there in a teaspoon of sugar?

   a. 15   **b.** 18   **c.** 20

3. One hour of walking at 2 miles per hour burns about as many calories as in which food?

   a. 1 cup of corn chips   **b.** 1 banana   **c.** 2 cups of cola

4. Which activity burns fewer calories than doing light housework?

   a. playing basketball   **b.** slow walking   **c.** fast bicycling

5. To burn the calories in two ounces of jelly beans, which activity could you do?

   a. slow bicycling   **b.** ballroom dancing   **c.** talking to someone

13 **Name the different classes of foods found on the food pyramid. Write the word(s) on the line.**

1. _____   2. _____   3. _____   4. _____

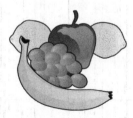

5. _____   6. _____   7. _____   8. _____

14 ▸**CHALLENGE** Look at the food pyramid and Victor Saiz's food record for today. How many servings of each food group did Mr. Saiz eat today? Write the number on the line.

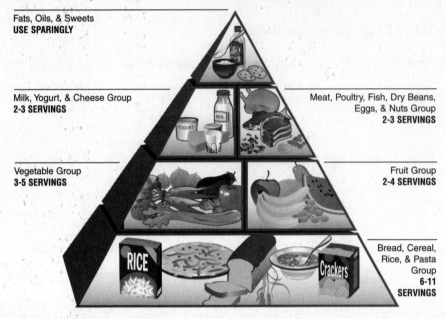

Breakfast	Lunch	Dinner	Snacks
bread – 2 slices 1 yogurt 1 egg 1 cup of milk 1 bowl of cereal	bread – 2 slices peanut butter – 1 tablespoon 1 apple 2 cookies jelly beans – 1 ounce	1 cup of rice chicken – 1 piece carrots – 1 cup chocolate cake – 1 piece	american cheese – 2 ounces ice cream

1. _____ grains   3. _____ vegetables   5. _____ dairy

2. _____ fruits   4. _____ meat   6. _____ fats/oils/sweets

15 Look at Mr. Saiz's food record again. According to the food pyramid, what should Mr. Smith have eaten? What should he not have eaten? Write sentences.

1. _Mr. Saiz should have eaten more vegetables._ _____

2. _____

3. _____

4. _____

UNIT 9

Your money

➤ Practical conversations

1 ➤ **VOCABULARY** Look at the pictures. Fill in the blanks with words from the box.

| cash machine | personal checks | credit cards | wallet | out of cash |

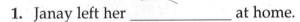

1. Janay left her _____ at home.

2. Do you take _____?

3. I'm completely _____. Can I borrow $5?

4. We need to go to the _____ before the movie.

5. That supermarket doesn't accept _____.

2 Put the conversation in order. Write the number on the line.

___*1*___ I'm collecting for a birthday cake for Patsy. Do you want to contribute?

_____ That's too bad. Would you like me to put in $5 for you?

_____ No problem.

_____ That would be really great. I'll pay you back tomorrow.

_____ Yes, but I'm a little short of cash right now. I left my wallet at home this morning.

___*6*___ Thanks. I really appreciate it.

3 ➤ *VOCABULARY* **Complete the sentences. Write the letters of each word on the lines.**

1. I'm working now, but my dream is to go to __ _r_ __ ◯ __ __ _t_ __ school.

2. Couldn't you try to get a __ _c_ __ __ __ ◯ __ _h_ __ __ __ ?

3. We now have a __ __ _r_ ◯ __ __ __   __ _n_ __ _o_ __ at work.

4. Maybe I could do it if I got a college __ _o_ ◯ __ . I'll call the bank tomorrow.

5. If I have to, I'll borrow ◯ __ _n_ __ __ __ from my family.

6. Do they offer tuition __ __ __ _s_ __ ◯ _t_ __ __ __ __ at your company?

Look at the circled letters. What's the new word? _____

4 **Offer advice. Complete each sentence.**

1. **A:** I'd like to open my own business, but I'd need a lot of money.

   B: Why don't you _____?

2. **A:** We've always wanted to buy a house, but it's so expensive.

   B: Why don't you _____?

3. **A:** I've always dreamed of visiting Egypt. I just don't have the money right now.

   B: Why don't you _____?

4. **A:** My wife's dream is to send both of our children to college.

   B: Why don't you _____?

5 **Complete the conversation. Use your <u>own</u> words.**

A: I've always wanted to _____, but it's so expensive.

B: Maybe you could _____.

A: I guess that's possible. Or I could _____.

B: That's right. It couldn't hurt to give it a try!

➤ Practical grammar

6 **Complete the sentences. Use words from the box.**

| they're | their | there | it's | its | then | than | your | you're | two | too | to |

1. I'm out of money. I'll have _____ stop at the ATM.

2. That's _____ problem, not my problem.

3. The community college has good teachers, and _____ tuition is much less _____ the university's.

4. _____ supposed to pay back _____ loan after you finish college.

5. Paulo borrowed $10 from me last week, and _____ yesterday he asked me for another loan.

6. If _____ not _____ expensive, I'd like to go on a cruise.

7. My relatives can't really help. _____ buying a house right now.

8. _____ are _____ applications you need to fill out. One is for a scholarship, and the other is for a loan.

7 **Complete the sentences. Write the letter on the line.**

1. Auto insurance is expensive, ___

2. There's no bus service near my office, ___

3. My dream is to finish college, ___

4. I'm not applying for a loan, ___

5. To pay for college, I'm working a part-time, ___

a. so I'm applying for a scholarship.

b. and I'm applying for a scholarship.

c. but I really need a car.

d. but I'm applying for a scholarship.

e. so I really need a car.

8 Combine the sentences with <u>and</u>, <u>but</u>, or <u>so</u>.

1. Reina applied for a car loan. She got it.

   _____

2. I get paid Friday. I can pay you back then.

   _____

3. The house is wonderful. It needs a lot of renovation.

   _____

4. I've always wanted to learn to swim. I'm taking lessons.

   _____

5. The car is in good condition. It's reasonably priced.

   _____

6. Victor would love to go to technical school. It's very expensive.

   _____

9 Read Mr. Njuma's story. Then answer the questions.

"When I joined the credit union, I got some information on loans. I didn't need a loan   then, so I didn't pay attention to it. Last month, I started thinking about buying a car. I looked for the loan information, but I couldn't find it. I stopped at the credit union on my way home from work, and I got another copy. Their rates are pretty good, so I'll probably apply for a loan there."

1. Why didn't Mr. Njuma pay attention to the loan information at first?

   _____

2. Why did Mr. Njuma visit the credit union today?

   _____

3. Why will Mr. Njuma apply for a car loan from the credit union?

   _____

10 Complete the sentences about <u>yourself</u>.

1. I've always wanted to _____, so _____.

2. I like _____ very much, but _____.

3. I can't afford _____ right now, so _____.

➤ Authentic practice

11 **Read. Choose your response. Fill in the ovals.**

1. "I can zap you over a copy by fax if you want."

   ⓐ OK. The number is 555-6984   ⓑ OK. I have e-mail.

2. "How many can I put you down for?"

   ⓐ Got it.   ⓑ 10, maybe 12.

3. "You'll need to provide your own equipment and mailing list."

   ⓐ Suit yourself.   ⓑ I'll need to give it some thought.

4. "The schedule is flexible, depending on how busy we are."

   ⓐ That's right up my alley.   ⓑ Can I send you a contract?

5. "Rates are probably going up after the first of the year."

   ⓐ I'd like to get rich quick.   ⓑ We'd better act fast.

12 **Read the conversation.**

Ed: Congratulations on the new car!

Bill: Thanks! I got a good deal on a loan, so I bought the car!

Ed: That's great. Which bank did you get the loan from?

Bill: Actually, I got it through the credit union.

Ed: Really? Why?

Bill: Well, their terms were better than the bank's, and the office is right here in our building. It's really convenient.

Ed: I know the credit union is there, but I've never checked it out.

Bill: Well, they also pay higher interest on savings accounts than at a bank, so I'm glad I joined. Any employee can.

Ed: That sounds like something I should try. Thanks.

Now complete the sentences. Write the answer on the line.

1. Bill got a new _____.

2. Bill got his car loan from his _____.

3. Ed is not a member of _____.

4. Bill likes the credit union because _____.

5. At Bill's company, any employee can _____.

13 Read the information on work-at-home schemes from a government Web site.

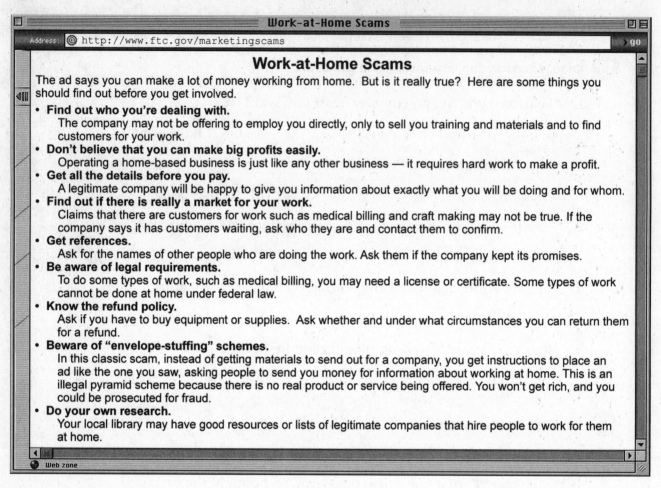

Now choose the correct answer. Circle the letter.

1. If a work-at-home company says that they already have customers for you, you should _____.

   a. write them a check   b. check with the customers   c. not believe it

2. Some work-at-home schemes require you to pay for _____.

   a. envelopes   b. a license or certificate   c. supplies or equipment

3. There are _____ for some jobs. You might need a license or certificate.

   a. legal requirements   b. refunds   c. references

4. It's a good idea to talk to other people working for the company to be sure _____.

   a. the company is reliable b. the people like   c. you can make
                                  what they do   a lot of money

5. Pyramid schemes are illegal because _____.

   a. they are classic   b. you could be prosecuted   c. nothing is being sold

14 Write three questions you should ask a work-at-home company. Use the information from the Web site.

1. _____

2. _____

3. _____

15 ▶ *CHALLENGE* Complete the paragraphs. Use words from the box.

finance	personal check	fee	after	paycheck	expires	before	pass

Leroy Adams is a little short of cash this month. His emissions inspection

_____ on April 8, and his car needs some repairs. Without the repairs, his car
    1.

won't _____ inspection. He needs $200 for the car repairs. Leroy won't get
       2.

his next _____ until April 15, so he is thinking about getting a payday loan.
      3.

If Leroy wants to borrows $200 from Kwik Kash King, he will have to give them a

_____ today for $200 plus a _____ of $30. Kwik Kash King will
    4.   5.

hold the check until his next payday. If Leroy pays back the loan _____
                                               6.

April 15, he won't have to pay any more fees. If he pays back the loan _____
                                                    7.

April 15, he'll have to pay a _____ charge.
                      8.

16 **Read the sentences. Then choose the word or phrase that is closest in meaning to the underlined word(s). Circle the letter.**

1. It's <u>awkward</u> to ask co-workers to pay back money, especially when it's a small sum.

   a. expensive   b. difficult   c. friendly

2. It's <u>inconsiderate</u> to keep borrowing money from a friend if you don't pay them back.

   a. thoughtless   b. nice   c. illegal

3. It's always good to <u>speak up</u>!

   a. speak loudly   b. say something   c. be quiet

4. The cost is <u>exorbitant</u>, and the yearly interest is more than 300 percent!

   a. very low   b. reasonable   c. very high

5. I learned <u>the hard way</u> that payday loans are not a good way to borrow money.

   a. this way   b. by making mistakes   c. by asking difficult questions

6. There are many <u>alternatives</u> to payday loans.

   a. other choices   b. other companies   c. other amounts

17 **Complete the sentences about borrowing money. Use your <u>own</u> words and ideas.**

1. If a woman in a parking lot asked me for $2 to take the bus home, I'd _____

   _____.

2. If a co-worker asked me for $10 and promised to pay me back on payday, I'd ____

   _____.

3. If I needed to borrow $150 because my paycheck was late, I'd _____

   _____.

4. If I needed $1,000 to open my own business, I'd _____

   _____.

5. If I needed to borrow $15 because I left my wallet at home, I'd _____

   _____.

6. If a friend borrowed money from me and didn't pay me back, I'd _____

   _____.

UNIT 10

Your career

➤ Practical conversations

1 **➤ VOCABULARY** Complete the sentences. Write the missing letters on the lines.

1. I'm looking for a bigger _c_ __ __ __ __ __ __ __ _e_ .

2. My English has really _i_ __ __ __ __ __ __ _d_ this past year.

3. I'll look for a new job when I _c_ __ __ __ __ __ __ _e_ my training class.

4. We had to move because my wife was _t_ __ __ __ __ __ __ __ __ __ __ _d_ .

5. Stacey is ready for a _c_ __ __ __ __ _r_ change.

6. There's not much _r_ __ __ _m_ to _a_ __ __ __ __ __ _e_ in this company.

7. I completed my _d_ __ __ __ __ _e_ last May.

2 Complete the conversation. Write the letter on the line.

A: Are you working now?

B: _____
   1.

A: How long have you been there?

B: _____
   2.

A: Do you like the work?

B: _____
   3.

A: OK. Why is that?

B: _____
   4.

A: I see. What would you like to do?

B: _____
   5.

A: That's great. Let's see what we can find for you.

B: _____
   6.

a. Well, there's not much room to advance where I am now. I'm ready for a bigger challenge.

b. Yes, I do. But I'm ready for a change.

c. Thanks. I appreciate it.

d. Yes, I am. I work at Ace Office Supply.

e. About a year and a half.

f. I was an accountant in my country, so I'd like to find a job in that area.

3 **Complete the sentences. Use words from the box.**

salary	tuition assistance	benefits	opportunities for growth
responsibility	perks	refuse	counteroffer

1. That company offers _____ for people in school.

2. I need health insurance for my family, so I'm looking for a job with

   _____.

3. She wants a job with more _____ than she has now as an assistant.

4. Liam has a lot of financial responsibilities. He needs a position with a higher

   _____.

5. When I told my boss about the offer, he made me a _____.

6. My company offers some nice _____, like free parking and bus passes.

7. Sujin got a job offer that was just too good to _____.

8. If you're interested in _____, we offer management
   training classes.

4 **Complete the conversation. Use your _own_ words.**

A: Hey, what's _____?

B: Well, you know I've been looking for another

   job because _____.

A: Yes, I know. Have you had any luck?

B: Actually, I've been offered a job.

A: Really? Where?

B: At _____.

A: That's great. Is it a good job?

B: Well, they're offering _____ and _____.

A: Sounds good. Have you made your choice?

B: _____.

➤ Practical grammar

5 **Complete each of the following past unreal conditional sentences.**

1. If they _had made_ me a counteroffer, I _would have stayed_ at the company.
   make   stay

2. If I _____ you were looking for work, I _____ you.
   know   call

3. I _____ up my mind sooner if I _____ more information.
   make   have

4. If Marina _____ her resume, it _____ a lot better.
   type   look

5. If I _____ there full time, I _____ eligible for benefits.
   work   be

6. Mr. Scopes _____ a letter of recommendation for Than if
   write

   he _____.
   ask

6 **Read the sentences. Then rewrite them as one past unreal conditional sentence.**

1. I stayed in school. I got my degree.

   If I hadn't stayed in school, I wouldn't have gotten my degree.

2. I took that job. I learned about working with customers.

   _____

3. Cindy spoke Spanish. She got the job.

   _____

4. Pedro knew how to do data entry. He got the promotion.

   _____

5. I was ready for a challenge. I applied for this transfer.

   _____

6. I didn't know there was an opening. I didn't bring my resume.

   _____

7 Write complete sentences. Begin with one word or phrase from each column. Finish the sentences with your own words.

If	I she he we you they	had hadn't	known about forgotten about seen told the boss about needed found	the mistake, the money, the e-mail, the resume, the terrible working conditions, the job announcement,

1. _If she had known about the mistake, she would have fixed it._

2. _____

3. _____

4. _____

5. _____

8 Complete the sentences about <u>yourself</u>.

1. If I hadn't studied English, _____

    _____.

2. If my family had _____ when I was young,

    _____.

3. If I hadn't moved here, _____.

➤ Authentic practice

9 **Read. Choose <u>your</u> response. Fill in the ovals.**

1. "Please forgive the interruption."

   ⓐ No problem. Come on in.   ⓑ I'll get back to you.

2. "If you'd be willing to hang in there till Friday, I'll see if there's anything I can do."

   ⓐ I'm not surprised.   ⓑ I appreciate it.

3. "If I'd known you were interested in a change, I'd have offered you something earlier."

   ⓐ Would you consider a counteroffer?   ⓑ It's not your fault.

4. "What about applying for a management position here?"

   ⓐ Actually, that never occurred to me.   ⓑ I've decided to take it.

5. "I understand you've been offered a position at a higher level."

   ⓐ Yes. It's just too good to refuse.   ⓑ You can take my word for it.

10 **Read the conversation.**

Dustin: Hey, Ted. Do you have a minute?

Ted: Sure. What's up?

Dustin: I was just wondering if you knew of any job openings where you work.

Ted: Hmm . . . Actually, I think one of my co-workers gave notice last week. Why?

Dustin: I'm ready for something new. I just can't make sandwiches forever. I need a bigger challenge.

Ted: I know what you mean. Have you talked to Richard?

Dustin: No, not yet. Why?

Ted: Well, he's a substitute teacher. The pay isn't great, but it's a professional job.

Dustin: That's true. And I do have some experience teaching back in Korea.

Ted: You should talk to Tim, too. He knows a lot of people, and he might have some ideas.

Dustin: OK, I will. Just keep your ears open and let me know if you hear about anything.

Ted: Sure. Hang in there!

Now choose the correct answer. Circle the letter.

1. What does Dustin want to do?

   a. make sandwiches

   b. change jobs

2. What does Dustin say he wants in a job?

   a. a bigger challenge

   b. a higher salary

3. What does Ted say about Richard's job?

   a. It's a professional job.

   b. The pay is great.

4. Why should Dustin talk to Tim?

   a. He has an open position.

   b. He might have some ideas.

5. What does Dustin ask Ted to do for him?

   a. Keep an eye out for any job opportunities

   b. Not to give up.

11 How important to you are these job features and perks? Rate the following by how important they are to you.

	Very important	Somewhat important	Not important
1. a high salary	❑	❑	❑
2. a lot of responsibility	❑	❑	❑
3. tuition assistance	❑	❑	❑
4. good benefits	❑	❑	❑
5. opportunities for growth	❑	❑	❑
6. good working conditions	❑	❑	❑
7. training opportunities	❑	❑	❑
8. challenging work	❑	❑	❑

12 Choose three features or perks that are important to you from the list in Exercise 11. Write sentences about why they are important.

1. _____ is important to me because _____

   _____.

2. _____ is important to me because _____

   _____.

3. _____ is important to me because _____

   _____.

13 **Read Tomas Slednik's employment history.**

Employment History

Company Name	Type of Business	Company Address	Phone Number
Parkland Properties	Apartment Complex Management Co.	480 Garden Blvd. Deerwood, MD 20788	(301) 555-3600

Starting Date		Leaving Date		Starting Base Salary	Final Base Salary	Starting Position Title	Last Position Title
Mo	Yr	Mo.	Yr			Maintenance worker	Maintenance crew supervisor
9	00			$ 325 (wk/yr)	$ 400 (wk/yr)		

Name of immediate supervisor ___Mr. Larry Tiet___   Supervisor's position title ___Owner___

Reason for leaving ___interested in professional employment___

Please describe your duties and responsibilities ___supervise crew of 6 performing maintenance and landscaping at large apartment complex; assign tasks, evaluate work, keep records___

May we contact that employer now? (Yes) No   If no, when? _____   Employer's Phone Number ___(301) 555-3626___

Company Name	Type of Business	Company Address	Phone Number
Landmark Linens	Commercial laundry	1550 Eagle Way Whitefish, MD 20781	(301) 555-2900

Starting Date		Leaving Date		Starting Base Salary	Final Base Salary	Starting Position Title	Last Position Title
Mo	Yr	Mo.	Yr			Laundry worker I	Laundry worker II
5	98	8	00	$ 200 (wk/yr)	$ 250 (wk/yr)		

Name of immediate supervisor ___Ms. Amina Karastolic___   Supervisor's position title ___Night shift supervisor___

Reason for leaving ___no opportunity for advancement___

Please describe your duties and responsibilities ___operated commercial laundry machines, sorted, folded and packaged linens___

May we contact that employer now? (Yes) No   If no, when? _____   Employer's Phone Number ___(301) 555-2980___

Complete the sentences about Mr Slednik.

1. Mr. Slednik got a job as a _____ at Landmark Linens in _____.

2. His final base salary at Landmark Linens was _____ a week. He worked
   there for about _____ years.

3. Mr. Slednik left his job at Landmark Linens because there were no
   _____ and his _____ had only gone up $50 a week.

4. In _____, Mr. Slednik started working at _____ as a
   _____.

5. His duties as a maintenance crew supervisor include _____
   _____.

6. Mr Slednik's current supervisor is _____.

14 **Read the article on resumes from *Modern Professional* magazine.**

Modern Professional

■ Tips for a winning resume

Before setting off on that job hunt, polish up your resume to showcase your strengths and make yourself irresistible to an employer. The two most popular formats for resumes are chronological and functional.

Chronological: Lists work experience and education in chronological order, with the most recent dates first. It is common to subdivide the information into categories such as "work experience," "education," "professional affiliations," "languages," and "awards."

Functional: Organizes the information by skill and accomplishment areas. These do not have to be arranged chronologically. The functional resume is most effective for persons wishing to change careers or for persons who have not been in the job market for a number of years.

Resume red flags

Don't put the following on your resume:

- salary information
- reasons for leaving jobs
- personal statistics (weight, height, health, marital status, children)
- names of supervisors
- names and addresses of references

Above all: **BE ACCURATE, TRUTHFUL, AND DON'T MISSPELL ANYTHING!**

Now check ☑ True or False.

	True	False
1. If you've been out of work for a while, a chronological resume is a good choice.	❑	❑
2. On a chronological resume, you should list your last job first.	❑	❑
3. A chronological resume should not include your schools and degrees.	❑	❑
4. You should have a good resume ready before you start job hunting.	❑	❑
5. You should include the names of your supervisors on your resume.	❑	❑
6. It's important to spell everything correctly on your resume.	❑	❑
7. A red flag is a warning of something you shouldn't do.	❑	❑

15 **Answer the questions about yourself.**

1. Which kind of resume would you write? Why?

_____

_____

2. Ask a friend or family member which kind of resume they would write and why? Write down their answer.

_____

_____

Skills for
test taking

Write your information in the boxes. Fill in the ovals.

LAST NAME	FIRST NAME	MI

(Bubble grid of letters A–Z for LAST NAME, FIRST NAME, and MI columns)

DATE OF BIRTH

Month	Day	Year 19__
Jan ○	⓪ ⓪	⓪ ⓪
Feb ○	① ①	① ①
Mar ○	② ②	② ②
Apr ○	③ ③	③ ③
May ○	④	④ ④
Jun ○	⑤	⑤ ⑤
Jul ○	⑥	⑥ ⑥
Aug ○	⑦	⑦ ⑦
Sep ○	⑧	⑧ ⑧
Oct ○	⑨	⑨ ⑨
Nov ○		
Dec ○		

TELEPHONE NUMBER

(Ten-column bubble grid with digits 0–9)

TODAY'S DATE

Month	Day	Year 20__
Jan ○	⓪ ⓪	⓪ ⓪
Feb ○	① ①	① ①
Mar ○	② ②	② ②
Apr ○	③ ③	③
May ○	④	④
Jun ○	⑤	⑤
Jul ○	⑥	⑥
Aug ○	⑦	⑦
Sep ○	⑧	⑧
Oct ○	⑨	⑨
Nov ○		
Dec ○		

Unit 1

Choose an answer.

Car wash for charity!

The Carlton High
School Helping
Hands Club is
sponsoring a car wash

Date: Saturday, June 2, and Sunday, June 3.
Time: 9:00 A.M.–4:00 P.M.
Place: 2500 Allen Drive
Cost: $5 for cars, $8 for SUVs and trucks

All proceeds will go to support Helping
Hands' programs for children, including
admission to parks and museums, after-
school snacks, and school supplies.

Don't drive around dirty!
Clean up for a good cause!

1. The Helping Hands Club is trying to
   raise money by _____.

   A. running a car wash
   B. running a bake sale
   C. selling school supplies
   D. selling cars

2. The money the club makes will be
   used for _____.

   A. a homeless shelter
   B. children's programs
   C. a scholarship fund
   D. a food pantry

1. Ⓐ Ⓑ Ⓒ Ⓓ

2. Ⓐ Ⓑ Ⓒ Ⓓ

Volunteer Opportunies

Union High School

Volunteers needed to tutor high school students in reading and math. One morning or afternoon a week; flexible schedule. Visit the school or call Rhonda at 555-3200.

Literacy Services of Jefferson County

needs volunteers (18 years or older) to help adults with basic reading, math, and English-speaking skills. Morning and evening schedules available. Call 555-1780.

Neighbor to Neighbor

Volunteers needed to drive home-bound senior citizens to medical appointments, friends' homes, and shopping areas. Reliable vehicle and good driving record required. Must be 18 years +. Call 555-8001; ask for Marit.

Friends of the Moosehead

Help with stream cleaning and litter removal on Saturday, March 23. Meet at the entrance to Moosehead Creek Park at 9:00 a.m. Old clothes recommended.

3. Which volunteer organization is looking for drivers?

A. Union High School
B. Neighbor to Neighbor
C. Friends of the Moosehead
D. all of the groups

4. What are the Union High School and the Literacy Services programs both looking for?

A. volunteers to teach English
B. volunteers to work in the afternoon
C. volunteers to make phone calls
D. volunteers to teach reading and math

5. Which agency is looking for volunteers for one day only?

A. Neighbor to Neighbor
B. Literacy Services
C. Friends of the Moosehead
D. Union High School

3. Ⓐ Ⓑ Ⓒ Ⓓ

4. Ⓐ Ⓑ Ⓒ Ⓓ

5. Ⓐ Ⓑ Ⓒ Ⓓ

Unit 2

Choose an answer.

Bradford Towers
Tenants' Association Meeting
Thursday at 7 PM
Community Room

Items to discuss:
- Management's proposed rent increases in January
- Broken locks on outside doors
- Door-to-door salespeople in buildings
- Slow response to phone outage emergency last week
- Testing for radon and lead paint: Who is responsible?

Your tenants' association needs you!
Dues are only $25 a year and go toward keeping
Bradford Towers a great place to live. Join today!
Hope to see you Thursday!

1. A. This is a flyer about asking for donations.
   B. This is a flyer about household emergencies.
   C. This is a flyer about a renters' meeting.
   D. This is a flyer about the terms of leases for apartments.

2. A. The phones were out last week at Bradford Towers.
   B. The cable was out last week at Bradford Towers.
   C. The lock on the community room door at Bradford Towers is broken.
   D. Apartments at Bradford Towers need to be cleaned.

1. Ⓐ Ⓑ Ⓒ Ⓓ

2. Ⓐ Ⓑ Ⓒ Ⓓ

City of Greenville
Tenants' Handbook

Some of the most common problems that arise between landlords and tenants are avoidable. Before you rent that new apartment or house, use this checklist to get your landlord-tenant relationship off to a good start.

❑ **Read your lease or rental agreement.**
Before you sign, make sure the lease doesn't include restrictions you can't live with. Note whose responsibility it is to make repairs or pay for damage.

❑ **Ask about the rules.**
Find out if there are any rules tenants must follow. For example, rules about parking restrictions, guest policies, or use of building facilities may not be included in the lease. Ask to see these in writing.

❑ **Get a copy.**
Insist on a written lease. Never agree to a spoken or informal lease. Always get a copy of any legal document you sign.

❑ **Be sure the terms of any security deposit are clear.**
Get it in writing. Know up front what the landlord may withhold your security deposit for. Be sure the agreement spells out how much time the landlord has to refund your deposit to you when you leave.

❑ **Take a look around.**
Inspect the apartment or house before you pay a security deposit. Keep a list of any area or appliance that is damaged, dirty, or in poor condition. You may want to take pictures.

---

3. Who is this handbook for?

   A. landlords
   B. renters
   C. repair people
   D. guests

4. What does the handbook say renters should never do?

   A. ask for a written lease
   B. get a signed copy
   C. pay a security deposit
   D. agree to a spoken lease

5. What should tenants do before paying a security deposit?

   A. rent an apartment
   B. pay for damage
   C. check for damage
   D. ask for a refund

---

3. Ⓐ Ⓑ Ⓒ Ⓓ

4. Ⓐ Ⓑ Ⓒ Ⓓ

5. Ⓐ Ⓑ Ⓒ Ⓓ

Unit 3

Choose an answer.

Morningside Police Department
Citation

☑ Moving violation   ☐ Parking violation

This citation is issued to:
Rhonda Murray

Vehicle Make & Model: *Ensign 200X*
License Plate: *CA883VL*   State: *NJ*
Color: *Blue*   Year: *2001*

Date: *11/18/03*
Time: *2:35*   ☐ A.M. ☑ P.M.

Violation   ☐ failure to stop at sign
               ☐ failure to yield at sign
               ☐ failure to signal a turn
               ☑ tailgating
               ☐ speeding

Officer: *M. Solano*

1. This is a _____.

   A. warning
   B. fender bender
   C. traffic ticket
   D. parking violation

2. The driver, Ms. Murray, _____.

   A. didn't stop at a stop sign
   B. didn't signal before she turned
   C. was speeding
   D. was following another car too closely

1. Ⓐ Ⓑ Ⓒ Ⓓ

2. Ⓐ Ⓑ Ⓒ Ⓓ

Dear Ricky,
    Sorry I'm not here. I saw that we were out of spare batteries, so I went to the store to get some.
    I had a little fender bender in the parking lot at work today. Someone sideswiped the car. He left a note with his name and number. There wasn't really any damage, but there's a scratch in the paint near the back left tire.
    Tanya's teacher called to talk about Tanya's grade in Spanish class. We need to talk to Tanya about doing her homework on time.
    Do you want to order pizza tonight instead of cooking? Call me on my cell phone and I'll pick one up. See you about 6:30.
                                    Love,
                                    Brenda

3. Why did Brenda go to the store?

   A. because she had a fender bender
   B. to buy batteries
   C. to get a pizza
   D. to buy a cell phone

4. What happened to Brenda's car today?

   A. She totaled it.
   B. She was in an accident.
   C. A man sideswiped it in the parking lot.
   D. A man hit her and didn't leave his name.

5. What is Brenda thinking about doing for dinner?

   A. getting a pizza
   B. going to a restaurant
   C. cooking
   D. making a Spanish omelette

3. Ⓐ Ⓑ Ⓒ Ⓓ

4. Ⓐ Ⓑ Ⓒ Ⓓ

5. Ⓐ Ⓑ Ⓒ Ⓓ

Unit 4

Choose an answer.

Check-Out Policy

If you left an imprint of your credit card when you checked in, or guaranteed with your card when you made your reservation, you may use our Express Check-Out procedure. For Express Check-Out, simply drop your key card in the Express Check-Out slot at the front desk. If you wish to see your bill, or if you are paying by check, please come to the front desk to check out in person.

Regular check-out time is 12:00 noon. Please contact the front desk if you need to make arrangements for a late check-out. If you need assistance with your luggage, please contact the bell office.

1. A. Guests can use Express Check-Out if they are paying by check.
    B. Guests can't use Express Check-Out if they check out before 12:00.
    C. Guests can't use Express Check-Out if they made a reservation.
    D. Guests can use Express Check-Out if they are paying by credit card.

2. A. Guests who need help with their luggage should contact the front desk.
    B. Guests who want to use Express Check-Out should contact the front desk.
    C. Guests who need help with their luggage should contact the bell office.
    D. Guests who want late check-out should contact the bell office.

1. Ⓐ Ⓑ Ⓒ Ⓓ

2. Ⓐ Ⓑ Ⓒ Ⓓ

Congratulations! You've won a fabulous dream vacation!

U.S. POSTAGE
H METER 123456

Congratulations! You've won a fabulous dream vacation for two at the Paradise Sands timeshare extravaganza. This all-inclusive vacation includes a chance to win one of hundreds of prizes in our Getaway raffle. Come experience paradise for yourself – white sandy beaches, clear blue water, and much, much, more!

To claim your prize, call (800) FUN4YOU. But you must hurry! Time is limited! Call and reserve your spot now before it's too late.

3. What is this letter about?

A. services in a hotel
B. a free trip offer
C. complaints about travel fraud
D. making reservations

4. What is this offer actually trying to do?

A. get someone to buy a timeshare at Paradise Sands
B. give someone a job at Paradise Sands
C. ask someone to contribute to a good cause at Paradise Sands
D. tell someone about housing discrimination at Paradise Sands

5. Why should the recipient of this letter call the phone number soon?

A. because the writer of this letter is in a hurry
B. because of the raffle
C. because it's an all-inclusive offer
D. because it's a limited-time offer

3. Ⓐ Ⓑ Ⓒ Ⓓ

4. Ⓐ Ⓑ Ⓒ Ⓓ

5. Ⓐ Ⓑ Ⓒ Ⓓ

Unit 5

Choose an answer.

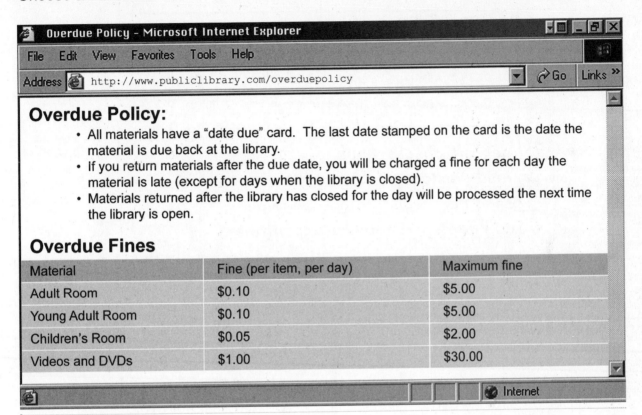

1. If you return materials to the library late, the fine you must pay gets larger _____.

   A. every day
   B. when the library is closed
   C. when the materials are processed
   D. every day the library is open

2. If you returned a book from the Children's Room five days late, the fine would be _____.

   A. $0.25
   B. $0.50
   C. $2.00
   D. $5.00

1. Ⓐ Ⓑ Ⓒ Ⓓ

2. Ⓐ Ⓑ Ⓒ Ⓓ

To Do

Priority key: A = Do it now!   B = Do if there's time   C = Do another day

A	call Tony about meeting tomorrow
A	reschedule appointment with Ned's teacher
A	order birthday cake from Neri's Bakery
C	return Debbie's cookbook
B	get birthday card for Diego
B	deposit checks—bank
B	mail package to Dad—post office
A	send car registration renewal!
C	call dentist and make appointment

3. Where does this person have to go today?

   A. to the bakery
   B. to Diego's birthday party
   C. to a meeting
   D. to Ned's school

4. What kind of appointment did this person miss?

   A. a dentist's appointment
   B. an appointment with a teacher
   C. an appointment at the auto repair shop
   D. an appointment at the bank

5. What will this person probably not do today?

   A. call Tony
   B. get a birthday card
   C. return a book
   D. order a cake

3. Ⓐ Ⓑ Ⓒ Ⓓ

4. Ⓐ Ⓑ Ⓒ Ⓓ

5. Ⓐ Ⓑ Ⓒ Ⓓ

Unit 6

Choose an answer.

The Town Herald • WEDNESDAY, MAY 12, 200

Storm hits metro area

A major spring storm hammered Highland Park yesterday evening. The storm, which caused major damage in several neighborhoods, came in unexpectedly early last night. Many people were driving home from work when the worst of the weather hit. "Visibility was really down — I couldn't see the car in front of me," one driver said. "I had to stop under an overpass until it cleared up. It took me two hours to get home." Other drivers were stuck for hours when their cars stalled after trying to make it through high standing water.

In one neighborhood, hundreds of homes were without electricity after the storm had passed through. HP Electric estimated that 750 customers were still without power at midnight. "We have crews out working as fast as they can," one HP official said, "but it may take a day or two before everyone's power is back on."

In other areas, downed power lines made crossing the street extremely dangerous. "All in all, we can thank our lucky stars," Mayor Adkins said. "There was a lot of property damage, but no one was seriously injured."

1. What happened in Highland Park yesterday?

   A. A storm caused a lot of problems.
   B. Everyone's power came back on.
   C. People were seriously hurt.
   D. 750 homes were damaged.

2. Why did the mayor thank his lucky stars?

   A. because there was property damage
   B. because the crews worked as hard as they could
   C. because the storm was over at midnight
   D. because no one was hurt

3. How many people didn't have electricity at midnight?

   A. less than 750
   B. exactly 750
   C. more than 750
   D. about 750

1. Ⓐ Ⓑ Ⓒ Ⓓ

2. Ⓐ Ⓑ Ⓒ Ⓓ

3. Ⓐ Ⓑ Ⓒ Ⓓ

Velela Household Painting
15678 E. Dakota Avenue, Denver, CO 80232
(303) 555-7838

Mr. and Mrs. Paul Mitchell
45 Plainview Court, Milton, CO 80231
Paint all sides of house with Silas Morton paints, 2 coats
Estimate: $4,500, including labor and supplies

Konstantanides Building Services
4597 Brenner Avenue, Milton, CO 80211

For Paul Mitchell, 45 Plainview Court
Paint house, 2 coats, $3,600 + labor

4. Mr. and Mrs. Mitchell live on
   _____.

   A. East Dakota Avenue in Denver
   B. Brenner Avenue in Milton
   C. Plainview Court in Milton
   D. Silas Morton Pt. in Milton

5. The Mitchells got _____
   from two different companies.

   A. insurance claims
   B. written estimates
   C. accident reports
   D. insurance polices

4. Ⓐ Ⓑ Ⓒ Ⓓ

5. Ⓐ Ⓑ Ⓒ Ⓓ

Unit 7

Choose an answer.

1. What does this flyer ask people to do?

   A. protest a peace march
   B. discuss the Bill of Rights
   C. discuss the pros and cons of capital punishment
   D. protest capital punishment

2. What is the opinion of the Pro-Justice Coalition for Peace about capital punishment?

   A. They are in favor of it.
   B. They are against it.
   C. They believe in it.
   D. They agree to disagree.

1. Ⓐ Ⓑ Ⓒ Ⓓ

2. Ⓐ Ⓑ Ⓒ Ⓓ

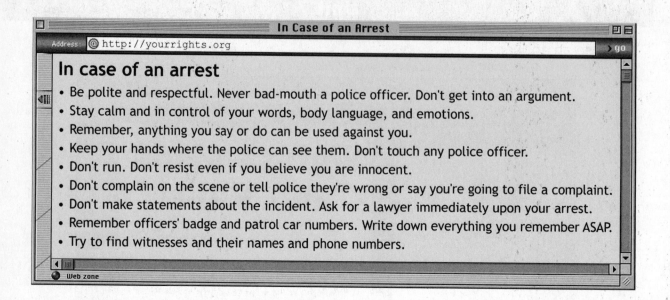

In Case of an Arrest

Address: @ http://yourrights.org › go

In case of an arrest

- Be polite and respectful. Never bad-mouth a police officer. Don't get into an argument.
- Stay calm and in control of your words, body language, and emotions.
- Remember, anything you say or do can be used against you.
- Keep your hands where the police can see them. Don't touch any police officer.
- Don't run. Don't resist even if you believe you are innocent.
- Don't complain on the scene or tell police they're wrong or say you're going to file a complaint.
- Don't make statements about the incident. Ask for a lawyer immediately upon your arrest.
- Remember officers' badge and patrol car numbers. Write down everything you remember ASAP.
- Try to find witnesses and their names and phone numbers.

Web zone

3. The Web site gives a list of
_____.

A. pros and cons
B. laws
C. controversial issues
D. recommendations

4. The Web site says that if you are
arrested, you shouldn't _____.

A. write anything down
B. try to find witnesses
C. resist or complain
D. file a complaint

5. According to the Web site, it's
important to get the phone numbers of
_____.

A. witnesses
B. police officers
C. lawyers
D. patrol cars

3. Ⓐ Ⓑ Ⓒ Ⓓ

4. Ⓐ Ⓑ Ⓒ Ⓓ

5. Ⓐ Ⓑ Ⓒ Ⓓ

Unit 8

Choose an answer.

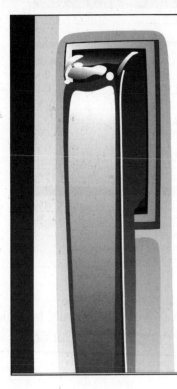

Tips to reduce fat and cholesterol
- Steam, boil, bake, or microwave vegetables instead of frying.
- Season vegetables with herbs and spices instead of butter, margarine, or fatty sauces.
- Try flavored vinegars or lemon juice on salads. Limit oil-based salad dressings.
- Replace whole milk with low-fat or skim milk in puddings, soups, and baking.
- Substitute plain low-fat yogurt or blender-whipped low-fat cottage cheese for sour cream or mayonnaise.
- Choose lean cuts of meat, and trim fat from meat and poultry before and after cooking. Remove skin from poultry before or after cooking.
- Cook meat or poultry on a rack so the fat will drain off. Use a non-stick pan for cooking so adding fat isn't necessary.

1. The article says you can reduce the amount of fat you eat with vegetables by _____.

   A. frying them
   B. not adding butter or margarine to them
   C. using oil-based salad dressings
   D. removing the skin before you cook them

2. You would use these tips if you wanted to _____.

   A. watch the amount of salt in your diet
   B. stay away from low-fat foods
   C. lower your blood pressure
   D. limit fat and cholesterol in your diet

1. Ⓐ Ⓑ Ⓒ Ⓓ

2. Ⓐ Ⓑ Ⓒ Ⓓ

2% Reduced-Fat Milk	
Nutrition Facts	
Serving Size 1 cup: (236ml)	
Servings Per Container: 1	
Amount Per Serving	
Calories 120	Calories from Fat 45
	% Daily Value*
Total Fat 5g	**8%**
Saturated Fat 3g	**15%**
Cholesterol 20mg	**7%**
Sodium 120mg	**5%**
Total Carbohydrate 11g	**4%**
Dietary Fiber 0g	**0%**
Sugars 11g	
Protein 9g	**17%**
Vitamin A 10% • Vitamin C 4%	
Calcium 30% • Iron 0% • Vitamin D 25%	
*Percent Daily Values are based on a 2,000-calorie diet. Your daily values may be higher or lower depending on your calorie needs.	

Nonfat Chocolate Milk	
Nutrition Facts	
Serving Size 1 cup: (236ml)	
Servings Per Container: 1	
Amount Per Serving	
Calories 80	Calories from Fat 0
	% Daily Value*
Total Fat 0g	**0%**
Saturated Fat 0g	**0%**
Cholesterol Less than 5mg	**0%**
Sodium 120mg	**5%**
Total Carbohydrate 11g	**4%**
Dietary Fiber 0g	**0%**
Sugars 11g	
Protein 9g	**17%**
Vitamin A 10% • Vitamin C 4%	
Calcium 30% • Iron 0% • Vitamin D 25%	
*Percent Daily Values are based on a 2,000-calorie diet. Your daily values may be higher or lower depending on your calorie needs.	

3. What is the serving size of both kinds of milk?

   A. 1 cup
   B. 1 container
   C. 2 cups
   D. 9 grams

4. Which kind of milk contains less cholesterol?

   A. 2% reduced-fat milk has less cholesterol.
   B. Nonfat chocolate milk has less cholesterol.
   C. They have the same amount.
   D. We don't know from the information given.

5. What part of your total daily fat value does a serving of 2% reduced-fat milk provide?

   A. 0%
   B. 8%
   C. 5%
   D. 45%

3. Ⓐ Ⓑ Ⓒ Ⓓ

4. Ⓐ Ⓑ Ⓒ Ⓓ

5. Ⓐ Ⓑ Ⓒ Ⓓ

Unit 9

Choose an answer.

Application for Financial Aid
Fill in completely. Use blue or black ink only.

Name: *Louis-Trent* _____ *Angelique* _____
            Last   First

Please check the type(s) of financial assistance you are applying for:
☑ scholarship   ☐ loan   ☑ work–study job

If you checked work–study job, how many hours a week can you work? _15_

Check type of higher education program you expect to enroll in:
☐ BA or BS degree program   ☑ AA, As, or AAS degree program
☐ graduate program   ☐ technical training program

Indicate month and year you expect to complete your degree: *May* *2005*
                                                    month   year

1. Ms. Louis-Trent does not want
    _____.

    A. financial aid
    B. a scholarship
    C. a loan
    D. a work–study job

2. Ms. Louis-Trent would like to go to
    college for _____.

    A. a BA degree
    B. an AA degree
    C. a graduate degree
    D. a technical school degree

1. Ⓐ Ⓑ Ⓒ Ⓓ

2. Ⓐ Ⓑ Ⓒ Ⓓ

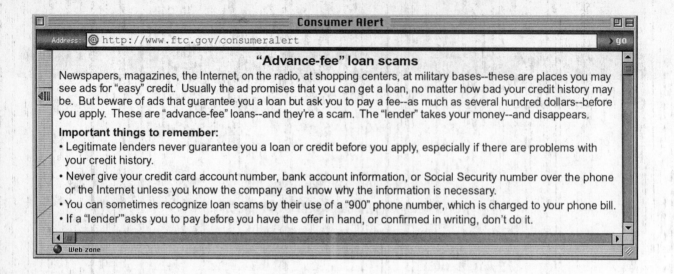

"Advance-fee" loan scams

Newspapers, magazines, the Internet, on the radio, at shopping centers, at military bases--these are places you may see ads for "easy" credit. Usually the ad promises that you can get a loan, no matter how bad your credit history may be. But beware of ads that guarantee you a loan but ask you to pay a fee--as much as several hundred dollars--before you apply. These are "advance-fee" loans--and they're a scam. The "lender" takes your money--and disappears.

Important things to remember:

- Legitimate lenders never guarantee you a loan or credit before you apply, especially if there are problems with your credit history.
- Never give your credit card account number, bank account information, or Social Security number over the phone or the Internet unless you know the company and know why the information is necessary.
- You can sometimes recognize loan scams by their use of a "900" phone number, which is charged to your phone bill.
- If a "lender"'asks you to pay before you have the offer in hand, or confirmed in writing, don't do it.

Web zone

3. According to this Web page, what is an advance-fee loan?

   A. a loan you must repay within one year
   B. a loan you must pay a fee for before you can apply
   C. a loan you can get through your credit card
   D. a loan you can get over the Internet

4. When is it OK to give your credit card number over the phone?

   A. when an ad guarantees you a loan
   B. when a lender asks you to pay in advance
   C. when the company has a "900" phone number
   D. when you know the company and why they need the information

5. Why are advance-fee loans a scam?

   A. because they are advertised at shopping centers
   B. because they charge the customer's phone bill for calls
   C. because they steal your money
   D. because customers who use them have a bad credit history

3. Ⓐ Ⓑ Ⓒ Ⓓ

4. Ⓐ Ⓑ Ⓒ Ⓓ

5. Ⓐ Ⓑ Ⓒ Ⓓ

Unit 10

Choose an answer.

Employment History

List all employment since high school, including summer, cooperative education, and U.S. military service (you need to provide dates and relevant duties only). Start with your most recent position. Periods of unemployment should also be noted. Leave no gaps in time sequence. If you need more space, please use an additional sheet of paper.

Last *Kwon*　　　　First *Poppy*　　　　M.I. *C*

List your current or most recent position here

Company Name and Address: *Shirley's Flowers, 298 Burnet St., Cincinnati, OH 45223*

Type of Business: *florist, flower delivery*　　　Phone Number: *(513) 555-2800*

Starting position: *delivery driver*　　　Employed from *3/00* to *present*

Most recent position: *flower arranger and shop clerk* Starting salary: *$4.75/hr.* Final salary: *$6.00/hr. (3/00-4/01)*

Immediate supervisor: *Ms. Shirley Bennett*　　　Supervisor's position: *owner / manager*

Duties and responsibilities *arrange flowers according to customers' orders, assist customers,*
　　take phone orders, make sales

Reason for wanting to leave: *limited opportunities for growth*　　May we contact this employer? Yes　No

1. How long has Ms. Kwon worked for her current employer?

   A. for two years
   B. since March 2000
   C. since June 2000
   D. since April 2001

2. What does Ms. Kwon do at her current job?

   A. She helps customers and arranges flowers.
   B. She owns and manages the shop.
   C. She grows and arranges flowers.
   D. She drives a delivery truck.

3. Why is Ms. Kwon looking for a new job?

   A. She wants to be a delivery driver.
   B. She wants better benefits.
   C. She wants more opportunities to advance.
   D. She wants tuition assistance.

1. Ⓐ Ⓑ Ⓒ Ⓓ

2. Ⓐ Ⓑ Ⓒ Ⓓ

3. Ⓐ Ⓑ Ⓒ Ⓓ

Francisco Canseco

12726 Woods Rd. Oakland, MI 48908

(517) 555-3102

OBJECTIVE

Responsible position as a medical technician in a hospital or clinic.

EDUCATION

Currently enrolled part time in BS nursing program at Wayne University.
AA in Nursing Technology, Oakland College, 2003.

EXPERIENCE

8/02 to present: Security guard   Oakland Schools, Oakland, MI
Provide security for a large public evening school.

5/99 – 8/02: Waiter and catering staff   Rise and Shine Inn, Oakland, MI
Served and cleared food for banquets and meetings; set up dining rooms.

3/98 – 5/99: Hotel housekeeper   Rise and Shine Inn, Oakland, MI
Cleaned hotel rooms; changed linens.

11/92 – 8/97: Village health worker   National Bureau of Health, Mexico
Taught health lessons to villagers. Prepared teaching materials.
Assisted in village clinic.

---

4. Mr. Canseco's resume lists his _____ job first.

   A. current
   B. first
   C. best
   D. favorite

5. Mr. Canseco is looking for a job as _____.

   A. a security guard
   B. a medical technician
   C. a nurse
   D. a housekeeper

4. Ⓐ Ⓑ Ⓒ Ⓓ

5. Ⓐ Ⓑ Ⓒ Ⓓ